MUSICIANSHIP FOR THE ELEMENTARY TEACHER
Theory and Skills through Songs

musicianship

FOR THE ELEMENTARY TEACHER

THEORY AND SKILLS THROUGH SONGS

Anne E. Pierce & *Neal E. Glenn*

The University of Iowa

McGraw-Hill Book Company

New York   St. Louis   San Francisco   Toronto   London   Sydney

MUSICIANSHIP FOR THE ELEMENTARY TEACHER:
Theory and Skills through Songs

49970

1 2 3 4 5 6 7 8 9 0 K P 7 4 3 2 1 0 6 9 8 7

This book is concerned with the basic musical information and skills necessary for teaching music to children. It is designed for the college student majoring in elementary education who lacks musical training and for the in-service classroom teacher who needs such aid. We have assumed that the book will be used in a course preceding one in general music methods or that it will supplement such a course. It is, therefore, not a methods book as such.

Music is worthy of the serious attention of mature students. Hence we have presented each topic on an adult level and have not made the work childlike in nature. Yet at the same time we have tried to avoid useless and confusing technicalities. In the authors' opinion, the right approach to theory and skills is through music itself. Therefore, in this text songs are the focal point of study. ese give esthetic experiences to parallel technical growth.

The book begins by providing a background of singing and listening be- musical notation and other technical phases are introduced. Against this ground, theory then is presented in a carefully planned sequence. At no are students expected to perform musical tasks for which they have not repared.

f students study each lesson conscientiously and review and apply wledge and skills frequently and regularly, at the close of the course they should have learned to use their voices musically and enjoyably, to deal with notational problems, and to play simple accompaniments satisfactorily. Furthermore, they will have acquired a repertoire of standard songs useful later in teaching children, and they will have gained practical musical information.

In addition to this book, a piano, keyboard diagrams, blank music paper, chromatic song bells, and Autoharps are essential. A large facsimile of the keyboard to place before the class is recommended. Rhythm instruments (such as rhythm sticks and drums) are desirable equipment, the number of each depending on the size of the class. Highly important is an efficient teacher. From the beginning, he should make each lesson stimulating, pleasant, and musically educational. At suitable times, he should play accompaniments to songs to enrich students' musical experiences. In each chapter, he should supplement and adapt the activities and assignments to the needs of his class.

We hope that this book will serve to open the doors to a world of music, the enjoyment of which will be constantly enhanced as students apply the skills and knowledge gained to the actual presentation of music to children.

Anne E. Pierce
Neal E. Glenn

preface

contents

𝒢 accompaniments 169

x

MUSICIANSHIP FOR THE ELEMENTARY TEACHER
Theory and Skills through Songs

Singing is undoubtedly the best means of bringing one into close contact with music. It provides a sound basis for learning musical theory and acquiring the musical skills necessary for teaching music to children. Perhaps some of you may say that you have had little or no experience in using your voice in song and that you "cannot sing." Nature, however, endowed most people with a vocal instrument which, with correct use, is capable of producing pleasant tones. Indeed, if you can speak with pleasing quality and can recognize differences in musical sounds, you usually can sing. It is not necessary that you have a beautiful voice, but it is essential that you *want* to sing and that you produce your voice freely and expressively.

This is not primarily a course in vocal training, but throughout the lessons you will sing many songs. When doing so, if you will follow the principles of correct singing, you will promote good vocal habits and overcome poor ones.

Principles of Correct Singing

posture

To sing well, you must have good posture. The body should be alert and erect, with chest comfortably up. Your head should be held naturally, with the chin at approximately a right angle to the throat. If there is space between the ribs and the hips, your position will generally be excellent. When standing, put your weight on the balls of the feet, with one foot somewhat in advance of the other so that your body is well balanced. Keep your knees straight. When sitting, place both feet on the floor, sit back in the chair, and then lean slightly forward.

breathing

If your posture is right, if your throat and facial muscles are free from constraint, if the song is within your singing ability, and if you render it musically and with enjoyment, you usually will breathe automatically and correctly. You should inhale deeply and quietly, never lifting your shoulders. When not using your voice, you should breathe through your nostrils, but when speaking or singing, you often need to take breath quickly through your mouth. When you exhale, do not let the body slump. The outgoing breath always should flow through a free, open throat so that the resulting tones will vibrate properly in the resonating cavities. When singing, as when speaking, you must know not only how to breathe and use the breath in the production of tones but also where to breathe. This is determined by the musical phrase and the meaning of the words.

phrasing

Phrases in music, as in poetry and prose, are units of thought.[1] Their lengths vary—some are short, some are long. Within a song, each phrase bears a relationship to the others; each has its points of climax and repose. At the close of phrases are pauses in the flow of music, called "cadences," which vary in conclusiveness. These are natural breathing points. But if the phrase is short and the pause that follows brief, the breath may be held over. However, if you do not have sufficient breath to sing an entire phrase, you then can replenish it

---

1. Phrases in most songs coincide with the lines of poetry.

at suitable places. The meaning of the sentences or the lines of poetry and their punctuation will guide you. You generally should not breathe between the syllables of a word, between an adjective and its noun, or between a subject and its verb. But to phrase a song well denotes more than taking breath in the right places. It means that you have stressed important words and syllables, that you have made tonal variations in quality (timbre) and intensity (dynamics), and that you have made gradations in rate of speed (tempo) so as to interpret intelligently and musically the author's and the composer's intentions.

diction

The manner of delivering words, known as "diction," is highly important in both speaking and singing. Diction involves correct pronunciation, distinct enunciation, and good tonal quality. In ordinary speech, there is little difference in the stress of vowels and consonants. In singing, however, the vowel is sustained. Consonants, which bring meaning to vowels, should be clear-cut and uttered quickly.[2] In forming words, the lips and tongue should be flexible. The jaw, too, should be devoid of stiffness so that the mouth can be opened the proper width. As a rule, the higher the pitch, the more open does the mouth become. But it should never be opened so wide that it is uncomfortable and impedes the free action of lips, tongue, and jaw. The tip of the tongue should lie forward in the mouth against the teeth or teeth ridge so that it does not interfere with the flow of tone and thus prevent good diction.

intonation

Intonation is the manner of singing a tone in regard to pitch. Singing "off pitch" or "out of tune" may result from uncertainty in singing, as for instance, when you are unfamiliar with the song. It may be caused by incorrect posture and breathing and tense throat and articulatory organs. It may be brought about by your state of mind and health. You may perhaps be nervous, have a cold, or be overly tired, or you may be disinterested in the song. Possibly the song is too taxing for your singing capabilities—the phrases may be too long, the intervals too difficult, or the range too extreme. Among other reasons for faulty intonation are the ventilation and the temperature of the room. In rare cases, imperfect hearing may be the source of the trouble. But usually, if you have an average musical ear and normally healthy vocal organs, intonation need not be defective. As a rule, if you cultivate a critical ear by listening closely to the pitch of tones in your own and other voices and in instruments and if you produce your voice freely, you will sing in tune.

expressive singing

In order to sing a song expressively, you must first gain insight into its words and music. Then you should try through appropriate tonal quality to color your voice so as to convey your feelings about the song to your listeners and make it significant to them. Your face should always reflect the moods of the song. But you should avoid mannerisms or affectation. If you are uncertain of your appearance when singing, practice occasionally before a mirror.

2. The consonants m and n, however, are sometimes prolonged.

Highly important in expressing the meaning of music is the rate of speed at which you sing. Indeed, tempo can affect the basic character of a song, changing a gay, joyous song or a quiet, subdued one in such a way that its true spirit is lost. Although each song has its own appropriate tempo, the tempo is by no means mechanical or inflexible. Accelerations at certain points and retardations at others are necessary for an artistic rendition. Important also is the amount of tone you use. You should not, for example, sing a lullaby with the same intensity as you would a lively song.

To help you interpret a song, composers and editors often include guides to the tempo and dynamics of a song in the form of certain words, frequently Italian, and symbols placed above the music. A few of those most commonly used are:[3]

Tempo

Accelerando (accel.)   *getting faster*
Adagio   *slow*
Allegro   *fast*
Allegretto   *moderately fast*
Andante   *a moderate walking tempo; a speed between* allegretto *and* adagio
Moderato   *moderate speed*
Moto   *motion;* con moto, *with motion*
Piu mosso   *in time, usually after slowing the tempo*
Presto   *very fast*
Rallentando (rall.)   *gradually slower*
Ritardando (rit.)   *getting slower (the same as* rallentando)

Dynamics and Expression

Crescendo (cresc., $<$)   *growing louder*
Decrescendo (decresc. or decr., $>$)   *growing softer*
Diminuendo (dim.)   *a gradual lessening in volume; same as* decrescendo
Forte (f)   *loud*
Fortissimo (ff)   *very loud*
Legato   *sustained, smoothly connected*
Maestoso   *majestic, stately*
Mezzo forte (mf)   *moderately loud*
Mezzo piano (mp)   *moderately soft*
Piano (p)   *soft*
Pianissimo (pp)   *very soft*
Sforzando (sf or sfz)   *strongly accented*
Sostenuto   *sustained*

3

Types of Voices

Voices are classified according to sex, namely, men's and women's, boys' and girls'. Further classifications are made with reference to age (children's and

3.   See glossary (Appendix D, pages 164–166) for a more complete listing of terms and symbols.

adults'), quality (timbre), and range. Men's voices, from the lighter and higher to the heavier quality and range, are termed tenor, baritone, and bass. Women's voices in the same order are soprano, mezzo-soprano, and contralto.

Children's voices are called treble or soprano because their range lies within the treble, or G, staff and because their quality resembles that of a mature soprano voice of light quality. Until adolescence, voices of boys and girls are similar in quality, but then the boy's larynx grows in such a way that the vocal cords lengthen and the pitch drops. The girl's larynx also changes, but the vocal cords do not lengthen to the same extent as do the boy's.

There are always marked individual differences within any classification and within any age group. For example, some singers with heavy, contralto quality have a higher range than do some sopranos; some young children may have a very limited range, whereas some may have an extensive singing compass. Quality and range develop with use and training in both children and adults.

The singing compass of children's voices in the elementary school (ages six to eleven) is usually about:

The average range of untrained adult voices is approximately:

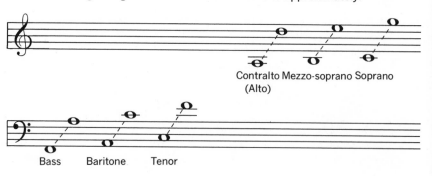

Singing Suggestions

Those of you who have not had practice in singing may find some notes in songs too high or too low to reproduce easily. If so, sing the notes with the vowel sounds *ah* and *oh* rather than the words. Try always, however, to sing all pitches of a song. Relax your jaw, have space between your teeth, open your throat as in a yawn, *think* and *hear mentally* the pitch, and then let the tone flow and resonate freely.

If you have difficulty in reproducing pitches accurately, or in common parlance, if you do not "carry a tune," find the pitch or pitches which you can produce easily and well. Usually this is within your speaking range. Sustain a tone on one of these pitches by singing words of one syllable such as *hoe, no, do, moon, hay, me, see, calm.* Sing the first and last phrases of "Now the Day Is Over" on the same pitch. When you can do this satisfactorily, sing the same words and phrases on lower and higher pitches. To inflect your voice in speech may prove to you that you have a useful vocal range.

Practicing certain parts of a song, such as the first part of "Joy to the

4

World'' and the last part of "Row, Row, Row Your Boat'' with vowel sounds and syllables such as *no, fa, la,* and *loo* on different pitches will help you increase both range and flexibility. To overcome sluggish use of lips and tongue, whisper or "lip" soundlessly the words of songs.

Assignment

1. Sing the following songs.[4] These are in a comfortable range for the average adult and child. Some of them doubtless are familiar to you. Your instructor will play and sing those which are unfamiliar until you know them.

NOW THE DAY IS OVER*[5]

Sabine Baring-Gould   Joseph Barnby

1. Now the day is o - ver, Night is draw - ing nigh;
2. Now the dark - ness gath - ers, Stars be - gin to peep;

Shad - ows of the eve - ning Steal a - cross the sky.
Birds and beasts and flow - ers Soon will be a - sleep.

Hum (*hm*) this melody with lips lightly together. Also sing it with lips slighty parted and the tip of the tongue against the back of the upper teeth ridge, producing the sound *hn.*

ALL THROUGH THE NIGHT*

Welsh

Quietly

1. Sleep, my child, and peace at - tend thee All through the night,
2. While the moon her watch is keep - ing All through the night,

Guard - ian an - gels God will send thee All through the night,
While the wea - ry world is sleep - ing All through the night,

Soft the drow - sy hours are creep - ing, Hill and vale in slum - ber steep - ing,
O'er thy spir - it gent - ly steal - ing, Vi - sions of de - light re - veal - ing,

I my lov - ing vig - il keep - ing All through the night.
Breathes a pure and ho - ly feel - ing All through the night.

---

4. If there are men in the class, they should sing naturally (an octave below the women).
5. An asterisk (*) on a song title indicates that there is an accompaniment to the song in Appendix G (pages 169–213). The symbol ' in the music is a breath mark.

5

JOY TO THE WORLD*

Isaac Watts

George F. Handel
Arranged by Lowell Mason

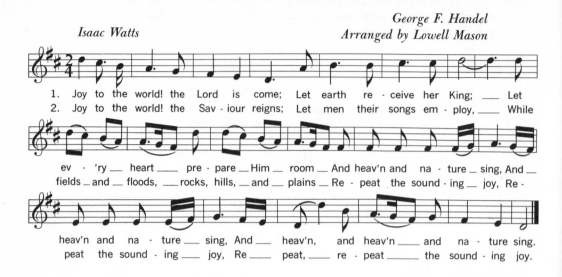

1. Joy to the world! the Lord is come; Let earth re · ceive her King; ___ Let
2. Joy to the world! the Sav · iour reigns; Let men their songs em · ploy, ___ While

ev · 'ry ___ heart ___ pre · pare ___ Him ___ room ___ And heav'n and na · ture ___ sing, And ___
fields ___ and ___ floods, ___ rocks, hills, ___ and ___ plains ___ Re · peat the sound · ing ___ joy, Re ·

heav'n and na · ture ___ sing, And ___ heav'n, and heav'n ___ and na · ture sing.
peat the sound · ing ___ joy, Re ___ peat, ___ re · peat ___ the sound · ing joy.

ROW, ROW, ROW YOUR BOAT

E. O. Lyte

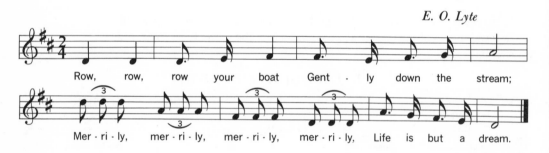

Row, row, row your boat Gent · ly down the stream;

Mer · ri · ly, mer · ri · ly, mer · ri · ly, mer · ri · ly, Life is but a dream.

THE BLUE BELLS OF SCOTLAND*

Annie McVicar

Old Scotch Air

1. O where, and O where is your High · land lad · die gone?
2. O where, and O where does your High · land lad · die dwell?

O where, and O where is your High · land lad · die gone?
O where, and O where does your High · land lad · die dwell?

He's gone to fight the foe for King George up · on the throne;
He dwelt in mer · ry Scot · land, at the sign of the Blue Bell;

6

And it's oh! in my heart how I wish him safe at home!
And it's oh! in my heart that I love my lad - die well.

VESPER HYMN*

Thomas Moore   *Attributed to D. Bortniansky*

Hark, the ves - per hymn is steal - ing O'er the wa - ters soft and clear.
Near - er yet and near - er peal - ing, Soft it breaks up - on the ear.

Ju - bi - la - te! Ju - bi - la - te! Ju - bi - la - te! A - _____ men.

Dots placed before the double bar (:||) mean that you are to repeat this section.

MAY DAY CAROL*

English Folk Song from Essex County

1. The moon shines bright, The stars give light, A
2. A - wake, a - wake, O pretty, pretty maid, Out

lit - tle be - fore it's day. Our Heav - en - ly Fa - ther, He
of _____ your drow - sy dream, And step _____ in - to your _____

called to us And bid us to wake and pray.
dair - y shed And fetch me a bowl of cream.

3. If not a bowl of your sweet cream,
   A cup to bring you cheer;
   For I don't know if we'll meet again,
   To be maying another year.

4. For I've been ramb'ling all this night
   And on into this day;
   And now, returning back again,
   I bring you a branch of May.

5. A branch of May I bring you here,
   As at your door I stand.
   'Tis but a sprout well budded out,
   The work of our dear Lord's hand.

6. My song is done, I must be gone.
   No longer can I stay,
   God bless you all, both great and small,
   And send you a joyful May.

7

SWEET NIGHTINGALE*

Allegro grazioso

Old English Air

1. Pret - ty maid, come a - long, Don't you hear the fond song, The sweet notes of the
2. Pret - ty Bet - ty, don't fail, For I'll car - ry your pail Safe____ home to your
3. Pray, ___ let me a - lone, I have hands of my own; A - ____ long with you,

night - in - gale flow? ___ Don't you hear the fond tale Of the sweet night - in -
cot as we go; ___ You shall hear the fond tale Of the sweet night - in -
Sir, I'll not go ___ To ____ hear the fond tale Of the sweet night - in -

gale As she sings in the val - ley be - low, _____
gale As she sings in the val - ley be - low, _____
gale As she sings in the val - ley be - low, _____

_____ As she sings in the val - ley be - low?
_____ As she sings in the val - ley be - low?
_____ As she sings in the val - ley be - low.

The symbol ⌒ (called the "fermata," or hold) means that you are to prolong the tone over which the symbol appears beyond its normal time value. The
exact length is determined by the character of the music and is at the discretion
of the performer or conductor.

SLUMBER BOAT*

Alice C. D. Riley

Jessie L. Gaynor

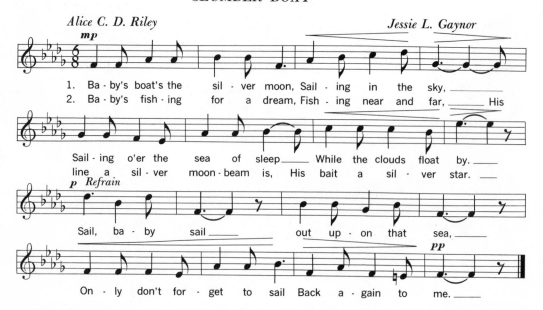

1. Ba - by's boat's the sil - ver moon, Sail - ing in the sky, _____
2. Ba - by's fish - ing for a dream, Fish - ing near and far, _____ His

Sail - ing o'er the sea of sleep_____ While the clouds float by. _____
line a sil - ver moon - beam is, His bait a sil - ver star. ___

p Refrain

Sail, ba - by sail _____ out up - on that sea, _____

On - ly don't for - get to sail Back a - gain to me. _____

DRINK TO ME ONLY WITH THINE EYES*

Ben Jonson   *Old English Air*

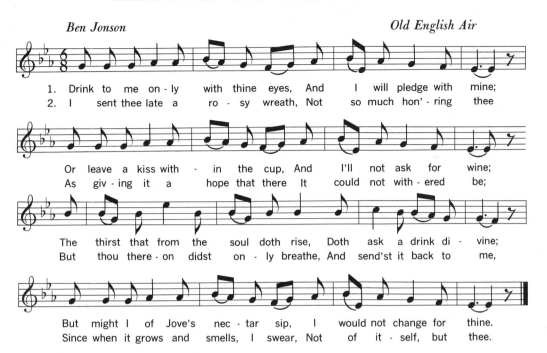

1. Drink to me on-ly with thine eyes, And I will pledge with mine;
2. I sent thee late a ro-sy wreath, Not so much hon'-ring thee

Or leave a kiss with - in the cup, And I'll not ask for wine;
As giv-ing it a hope that there It could not with-ered be;

The thirst that from the soul doth rise, Doth ask a drink di - vine;
But thou there-on didst on - ly breathe, And send'st it back to me,

But might I of Jove's nec - tar sip, I would not change for thine.
Since when it grows and smells, I swear, Not of it - self, but thee.

O REST IN THE LORD*6

Adapted from Psalm XXXVII   *Felix Mendelssohn*

Slowly

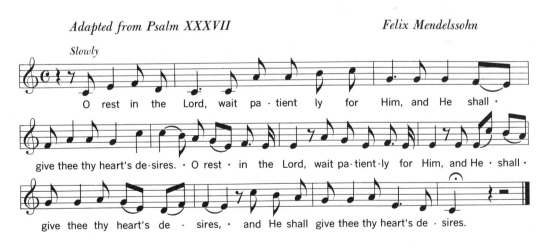

O rest in the Lord, wait pa - tient ly for Him, and He shall ·

give thee thy heart's de-sires. · O rest · in the Lord, wait pa-tient-ly for Him, and He · shall ·

give thee thy heart's de - sires, · and He shall give thee thy heart's de - sires.

In the following song, as each object is named in each stanza, those named previously are repeated in reverse order until the song is completed. Sing the measures marked 1 (⌐1.⎯⎯⎯⎯⎯⎤) for the first verse. Omit these for successive verses and sing the measures marked 2 (⌐2.⎯⎯⎯⎯⎤).

6. This is an excerpt from the famous aria for contralto voice from the oratorio *Elijah*. The complete version is in Appendix G (page 177).

THE TREE IN THE WOOD*

English Folk Song

1. All in a wood there grew a tree, The fin - est tree you ev - er did see,
2. And on this tree there grew a limb, The fin - est limb you

And the green leaves grew a - round, a - round, a - round, And the green leaves grew a - round.

ev - er did see; The limb was on the tree, The tree was in the wood,

Refrain

And the green leaves grew a - round, a - round, a - round, And the green leaves grew a - round.

3. And on this limb there was a branch,
The finest branch you ever did see;
The branch was on the limb,
    The limb was on the tree,
    The tree was in the wood,
And the green leaves grew all around, etc.

4. And on this branch there was a nest, etc.
5. And in this nest there was an egg, etc.
6. And in this egg there was a bird, etc.
7. And on this bird there was a wing, etc.
8. And on this wing there was a feather, etc.

2. After singing the foregoing songs, select four to memorize and sing as solos before the class.

3. Supply interpretative guides for the songs.

4. a Practice the singing suggestions given on pages 4 and 5.
    b Select portions of other songs you think would be suitable for vocalises.

5. After hearing different individuals in the class sing, classify their voices as to type. Classify your own voice.

6. Summarize the principles of correct singing.

7. Appraise the application of these principles in your own singing as well as in the singing of other individuals in the class and of the class as a whole.

The Structure of Songs

It will help you in your study of musical theory and music reading, as well as in your understanding and enjoyment of music, if you will learn to listen carefully to the various tonal sequences and observe the way they appear in a song.

Even the simplest musical composition has design, or pattern, frequently referred to as its "form." Form in music implies that the composer has followed certain principles found in all works of art—unity, contrast, climax, balance, and proportion. However, the word "form" is also used in a musically broader and historical sense. For example, the art song, madrigal, chorale, cantata, opera, oratorio, sonata, concerto, and symphony are forms *of* music and should be distinguished from forms *in* music with which you are concerned here. In studying the form *in* a composition, your musical memory is important, because you must recall the parts of a song and then combine these parts into a unified whole.

As you sang the songs in the preceding chapter, you found that there are phrases in music just as there are in prose and poetry. Now notice how these musical phrases are divided, combined, repeated, and varied. You will find that within a phrase are small distinctive groups of tones; these are called "motives."[1] They are developed into a phrase, then into a musical sentence, and finally into a complete song.

The first phrase of a song may sometimes sound incomplete and give a feeling of more to follow. It is called the "antecedent" phrase, or the "thesis." The second phrase, ending with a full or complete cadence, gives a feeling of finality. It is called the "consequent" phrase, or "antithesis." These two phrases make a musical sentence or period.

OLD FOLKS AT HOME

Stephen C. Foster

Antecedent phrase

Motive	Motive, Cadence
Way down upon the Swanee river,	Far, far away

Consequent phrase

Motive	Motive	Cadence
There's where my heart is turning ever,	There's where the old folks stay.	

These two phrases of "Old Folks at Home" constitute a musical sentence or period (sometimes called a double phrase). Roman numerals are used to indicate musical periods or sentences.

1. A motive may constitute a phrase, or it may be only part of a phrase.

OLD FOLKS AT HOME*

Stephen C. Foster

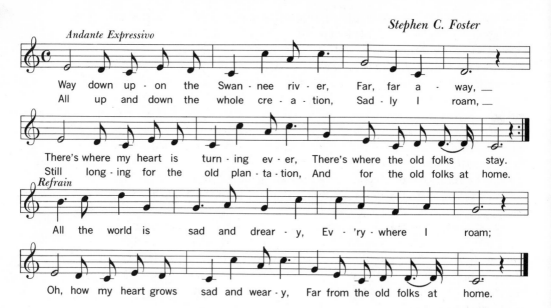

Way down up-on the Swan-nee riv-er, Far, far a-way, —
All up and down the whole cre-a-tion, Sad-ly I roam, —

There's where my heart is turn-ing ev-er, There's where the old folks stay.
Still long-ing for the old plan-ta-tion, And for the old folks at home.

Refrain

All the world is sad and drear-y, Ev-'ry-where I roam;

Oh, how my heart grows sad and wear-y, Far from the old folks at home.

The first phrase of a melody (the antecedent) and the second phrase (the consequent) are usually of the same length. However, there are exceptions. In the song "America," for example, which consists of two phrases, the first is shorter than the second.

AMERICA*

Samuel Francis Smith

Henry Carey

1st phrase

1. My coun-try, 'tis of thee, Sweet land of lib-er-ty, Of thee I
2. My na-tive coun-try, thee, Land of the no-ble free, Thy name I

2nd phrase

sing; Land where my fa-thers died, Land of the Pil-grims' pride,
love; I love thy rocks and rills, Thy woods and tem-pled hills,

From ev-'ry moun-tain-side, Let free-dom ring.
My heart with rap-ture thrills Like that a-bove.

12

3. Let music swell the breeze,
And ring from all the trees
Sweet freedom's song;
Let mortal tongues awake,
Let all that breathe partake,
Let rocks their silence break,
The sound prolong.

4. Our fathers' God, to Thee,
Author of liberty,
To Thee we sing;
Long may our land be bright
With freedom's holy light;
Protect us by Thy might,
Great God, our King.

Binary and Ternary Song Forms

By using letters you can indicate the number of phrases in a song and the way they are arranged. As a rule, songs have either two parts, a "question and answer" formation (AB), or three, a "statement, departure, and return" pattern (ABA). Those with two phrases (AB) are termed "binary," or two-part form, and those with three phrases (ABA) are "ternary," or three-part form.[2] In some songs, phrases are repeated, as AABBA or AABA, but this does not alter the form of the song. Sometimes the repeated phrase differs only slightly from the original. You can indicate this by placing a small mark after the letter representing the repeated phrase, as AA', BB'.

LITTLE BO-PEEP

Nursery Rhyme   J. W. Elliott

A   Lit - tle Bo - Peep has lost her sheep And can't tell where to find them;

B   Leave them a - lone and they'll come home, Wag - ging their tails be - hind them.

TWINKLE, TWINKLE, LITTLE STAR

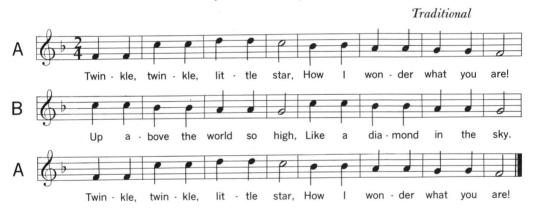

Traditional

A   Twin - kle, twin - kle, lit - tle star, How I won - der what you are!

B   Up a - bove the world so high, Like a dia - mond in the sky.

A   Twin - kle, twin - kle, lit - tle star, How I won - der what you are!

Irregular Forms

Some songs do not conform to the usual AB and ABA patterns. For example, some are ABACA, some are ABCA, and so forth. Only by careful observation will you discover how a composer deals with tonal material to give a song musical coherence, variety, and interest.

13

Assignment

1. As you sing the following songs, move your right arm from left to right in the form of an arc (⌒) with each phrase. Next, draw the arcs on the chalkboard or

2. You occasionally may find short songs for children with only one musical idea. These are "unitary," or one-part form.

a piece of paper as you sing. Indicate the phrase pattern by placing letters before each arc.

> "Blue Bells of Scotland"
> "Vesper Hymn"
> "Drink to Me Only with Thine Eyes"

2. In which of the following songs does the first phrase sound incomplete?

> "Now the Day Is Over"
> "All through the Night"
> "Row, Row, Row Your Boat"
> "May Day Carol"
> "Slumber Boat"
> "Little Bo-Peep"

3. Explain the following terms: binary, ternary, motive, period. Give specific illustrations.

4. After singing the following songs, decide the number and arrangement of phrases in each. Indicate motives and periods in three of these songs.

SUSIE, LITTLE SUSIE

German Folk Song
from Hansel and Gretel

1. Su - sie, lit - tle Su - sie, now what is the news? The geese are go - ing
2. Su - sie, lit - tle Su - sie, some pen - nies, I pray, To buy a lit - tle

bare - foot be - cause they've no shoes. The cob - bler has leath - er but
sup - per of sug - ar and whey. I'll sell my nice bed and go

no last to use, So he can - not make them a pair of new shoes.
sleep on some straw; Feath - ers will not tick - le, and mice will not gnaw.

THE LITTLE SANDMAN*

Johannes Brahms

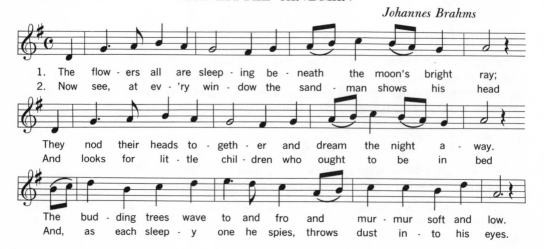

1. The flow - ers all are sleep - ing be - neath the moon's bright ray;
2. Now see, at ev - 'ry win - dow the sand - man shows his head

They nod their heads to - geth - er and dream the night a - way.
And looks for lit - tle chil - dren who ought to be in bed

The bud - ding trees wave to and fro and mur - mur soft and low.
And, as each sleep - y one he spies, throws dust in - to his eyes.

Sleep · on, sleep · on, sleep on, my lit - tle one.

OH, SUSANNA

Stephen Collins Foster

Brightly

I ___ came from Al - a - bam - a with my ban - jo on my knee,
It ___ rained all night the day I left, the weath - er it was dry,

I'm going to Louis - i - an - a, my ___ true love for to see.
The ___ sun so hot I froze to death, Su - san - na, don't you cry.

Oh, Su - san - na, oh, don't you cry for me,

For I came from Al - a - bam - a with my ban - jo on my knee.

SHE'LL BE COMING 'ROUND THE MOUNTAIN

Anonymous   *Southern Work Song*

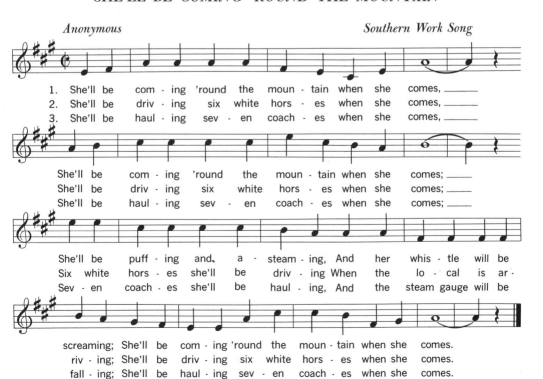

1. She'll be com - ing 'round the moun - tain when she comes, ___
2. She'll be driv - ing six white hors - es when she comes, ___
3. She'll be haul - ing sev - en coach - es when she comes, ___

She'll be com - ing 'round the moun - tain when she comes; ___
She'll be driv - ing six white hors - es when she comes; ___
She'll be haul - ing sev - en coach - es when she comes; ___

She'll be puff - ing and, a - steam - ing, And her whis - tle will be
Six white hors - es she'll be driv - ing When the lo - cal is ar -
Sev - en coach - es she'll be haul - ing, And the steam gauge will be

screaming; She'll be com - ing 'round the moun - tain when she comes.
riv - ing; She'll be driv - ing six white hors - es when she comes.
fall - ing; She'll be haul - ing sev - en coach - es when she comes.

15

FLOW GENTLY, SWEET AFTON*

Robert Burns   James E. Spilman

1. Flow gen - tly, sweet Af - ton, a - mong thy green braes; Flow
2. How lof - ty, sweet Af - ton, thy neigh - bor - ing hills, Far
3. Thy crys - tal stream, Af - ton, how love - ly it glides, And

gen - tly, I'll sing thee a song in thy praise; My
mark'd with the cours - es of clear wind - ing rills! There
winds by the cot where my Ma - ry re - sides! How

Ma - ry's a - sleep by thy mur - mur - ing stream, Flow
dai - ly I wan - der, as morn ris - es high, My
wan - ton thy wa - ters her snow - y feet lave, As,

gen - tly, sweet Af - ton, dis - turb not her dream. Thou
flocks and my Ma - ry's sweet cot in my eye. How
gath - 'ring sweet flow - 'rets, she stems thy clear wave! Flow

stock dove, whose ech - o re - sounds from the hill, Ye
pleas - ant thy banks and green val - leys be - low, Where
gen - tly, sweet Af ton, a - mong thy green braes, Flow

wild whist - ling black - birds in yon thor - ny dell, Thou
wild in the wood - lands the prim - ros - es blow! There
gen - tly, sweet riv - er, the theme of my lays; My

green crest - ed lap wing, thy scream - ing for - bear; I
oft, as mild eve - ning creeps o - ver the lea, The
Ma - ry's a - sleep - by thy mur - mur - ing stream, Flow

charge you, dis - turb not my slum - ber - ing fair.
sweet scent - ed birk shades my Ma - ry and me.
gen - tly, sweet Af - ton, dis - turb not her dream.

16

GOD REST YOU MERRY, GENTLEMEN*

Traditional   *English Carol*

1. God rest you mer - ry, gen - tle - men, Let noth - ing you dis - may,
2. In Beth - le - hem, in Jew - ry, This bless - ed Babe was born,

Re - mem - ber Christ, our Sav - iour, Was born on Christ - mas Day
And laid with - in a man - ger, Up - on this bless - ed morn;

To save us all from Sa - tan's pow'r When we were gone a - stray.
The which His moth - er Ma - ry Did noth - ing take in scorn.

Chorus

O ____ tid - ings of com - fort and joy, com - fort and

joy, O ____ tid - ings of com - fort and joy.

Elements of Music

Tones are the raw material of music. It is only when they are arranged in a logical and meaningful way, however, that they make music. Their horizontal order is *melody,* the way they move is *rhythm,* and their vertical combination is *harmony.* These are fundamental elements of music and are closely related. Your attention, though, will be directed first to melody and rhythm and later to harmony, because harmony is the more sophisticated element.

Melody

Melody is not only a distinctive but also a popular part of music. In truth, if you try to recall any song with which you are familiar, you probably will think first of its melody. Although melodies differ from one another, in all you will find that brief periods of silence, or "rests," occasionally occur between groups of tones and that the distance or interval between them varies. Sometimes a tone moves nearby or stepwise to another, sometimes it skips or jumps to a higher or to a lower one, and at times it is repeated. This movement of pitch greatly influences the mood or character of a melody and gives it definite shape, often referred to as the "melodic line" or "melodic curve."

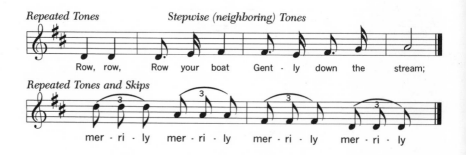

You can illustrate clearly the pattern of pitches by movements of your hands and by lines placed on the chalkboard or paper. A line picture of the first phrase of "Wait for the Wagon" would appear thus:

— —   — —

             — — —   — — — — — — —

The first phrase of "The Dairy Maids" would be:

— — — — —

             — — — — — —

WAIT FOR THE WAGON

R. B. Buckley

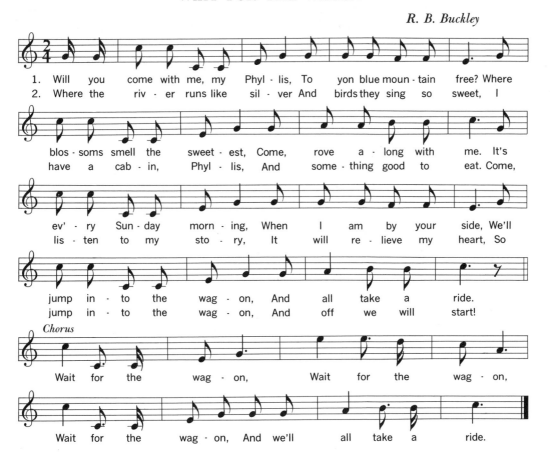

1. Will you come with me, my Phyl - lis, To yon blue moun - tain free? Where
2. Where the riv - er runs like sil - ver And birds they sing so sweet, I

blos - soms smell the sweet - est, Come, rove a - long with me. It's
have a cab - in, Phyl - lis, And some - thing good to eat. Come,

ev' - ry Sun - day morn - ing, When I am by your side, We'll
lis - ten to my sto - ry, It will re - lieve my heart, So

jump in - to the wag - on, And all take a ride.
jump in - to the wag - on, And off we will start!

Chorus

Wait for the wag - on, Wait for the wag - on,

Wait for the wag - on, And we'll all take a ride.

THE DAIRY MAIDS

Old English Song

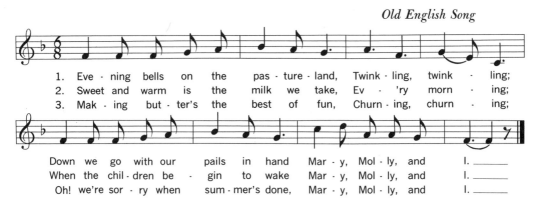

1. Eve - ning bells on the pas - ture - land, Twink - ling, twink - ling;
2. Sweet and warm is the milk we take, Ev - 'ry morn - ing;
3. Mak - ing but - ter's the best of fun, Churn - ing, churn - ing;

Down we go with our pails in hand Mar - y, Mol - ly, and I. _____
When the chil - dren be - gin to wake Mar - y, Mol - ly, and I. _____
Oh! we're sor - ry when sum - mer's done, Mar - y, Mol - ly, and I. _____

19

Rhythm

In paying close attention to the phrase and pitch patterns of a song, you cannot possibly avoid being aware of the way the music flows. In fact, you cannot dis-associate a melody from its movement.

This movement of music is known as its rhythm. The term is derived from the Greek word meaning "to flow." It is movement marked by repeated pulses, or accents. Although an indispensable element of music, rhythm exists apart from it. For example, there is rhythm in the beating of your heart, in the normal inhalation and exhalation of breath, in quick running steps and in the slower steps of walking, in the ticking of a clock, in the chug of an engine, and in the coming and going of the tides.

Rhythmic Grouping

In its movement, music tends to group into patterns of strong beats and beats less strong. These groupings form the meter of music. Simple meters are two, or duple (1 2); three, or triple (1 2 3); and four, or quadruple (1 2 3 4). Music which groups into beats of six is considered compound duple meter: two strong beats, each followed by two weaker beats (1 2 3 4 5 6).[1]

By calling the strongest-accented beat *one* whenever it occurs, you can readily count the weaker beats which follow. You can also clap your hands, tap your feet, strike a drum, and tap rhythm sticks to show how you feel the basic pulsation of the music. In addition, you can move your hand and arm as a musical conductor does.

When a song groups in beats of two, the movement of your hand and arm (the conductor's beat) is down on *one* (the strong accent) and up on *two* (the weaker accent).

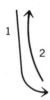

When music swings in groups of three beats, the movement is *down* (the strong beat), *right*, and *up* (the two weaker beats which follow).[2]

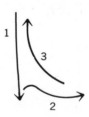

When music groups in four beats, there is a primary accent on one and a secondary accent on three (1 2 3 4), and the movement is *down, left, right, up.*

---

1. Simple meters multiplied by three form compound meters, such as six (compound duple), nine (compound triple), and twelve (compound quadruple). The nine and twelve meters occur infrequently in elementary school music books.

2. These directions are for the right-handed person. For a left-handed person, the directions are reversed (*down, left, up,* etc.).

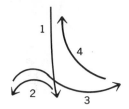

In songs where the grouping is in six (two groupings of three), the movement of the hand and arm is *down, left, left, right, right,* and *up.*

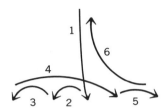

Melodic Rhythm

Melodies usually do not conform precisely to regular beats, one tone to each beat, but have tones of different lengths superimposed over the basic accents. This irregular rhythm gives interesting individuality to compositions. Indeed, you can recognize many familiar songs merely from hearing their melodic rhythm, for as Daniel Gregory Mason once wrote, "The rhythm is the face of each tune by which we know it."[3]

Row, Row, Row Your Boat

Melodic rhythm

Basic beats

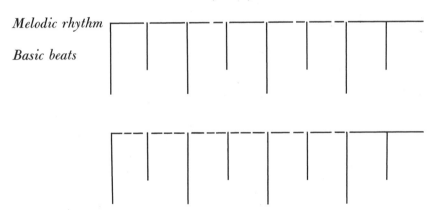

Expressiveness of Rhythm

Rhythm infuses music with life and is indispensable to the significance of a song. Usually, if accents are strong, the music is forceful and lively. On the other hand, music with light accents is quiet and restful. For example, the pitch patterns and movement of "The Star-Spangled Banner" are vigorous, whereas the

3. Daniel Gregory Mason, *A Guide to Music, The Appreciation of Music Series,* vol. 5, The H. W. Gray Company, New York, sole agents for Novello and Co., Ltd., London, 1905, p. 38.

melody and rhythm of Brahms' "Lullaby" are tranquil, the tune and rhythm of "Dixie" are rollicking, and the "Evening Song" has a calm movement.

THE STAR-SPANGLED BANNER*

Francis Scott Key

John Stafford Smith

1. Oh, ____ say! can you see, ____ by the dawn's ear · ly light,
2. On the shore, dim · ly seen ____ through the mists of the deep,
3. Oh, ____ thus be it ev · er when free · men shall stand

What so proud · ly we hail'd at the twi · light's last gleam · ing,
Where the foe's haugh · ty host in dread si · lence re · po · ses,
Be · tween their loved homes and the war's des · o · la · tion!

Whose broad stripes and bright stars, through the per · il · ous fight,
What is that which the breeze, o'er the tow · er · ing steep,
Blest with vic · t'ry and peace, may the heav'n - res · cued land

O'er the ram · parts we watch'd were so gal · lant · ly stream · ing?
As it fit · ful · ly blows, half con · ceals, half dis · clos · es?
Praise the Pow'r that hath made and pre · served us a na · tion!

And the rock · ets' red glare, the bombs burst · ing in air,
Now it catch · es the gleam of the morn · ing's first beam,
Then ____ con · quer we must, for our cause it is just,

Gave ____ proof through the night ____ that our flag was still there.
In full glo · ry re · flect · ed now ____ shines on the stream.
And ____ this be our mot · to: "In ____ God is our trust."

Oh, ____ say, does that ____ Star · Span · gled Ban · ner ____ yet ____ wave ____
'Tis the Star · Span · gled ____ Ban · ner! Oh, long may ____ it ____ wave ____
And the Star · Span · gled ____ Ban · ner in tri · umph shall ____ wave ____

O'er the land ____ of the free and the home of the brave?
O'er the land ____ of the free and the home of the brave!
O'er the land ____ of the free and the home of the brave!

22

LULLABY*

Johannes Brahms

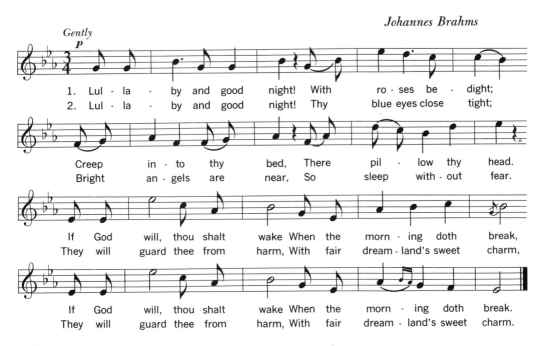

Gently
p

1. Lul - la - by and good night! With ro - ses be - dight;
2. Lul - la - by and good night! Thy blue eyes close tight;

Creep in - to thy bed, There pil - low thy head.
Bright an - gels are near, So sleep with - out fear.

If God will, thou shalt wake When the morn - ing doth break,
They will guard thee from harm, With fair dream - land's sweet charm,

If God will, thou shalt wake When the morn - ing doth break.
They will guard thee from harm, With fair dream - land's sweet charm.

The small notes are appoggiatura notes (from the Italian *appoggiare*, meaning "to lean" or "to rest"). They are to be sung quickly. Sometimes they are called "grace notes," for they serve to ornament a melody.

DIXIE*

Daniel Emmett

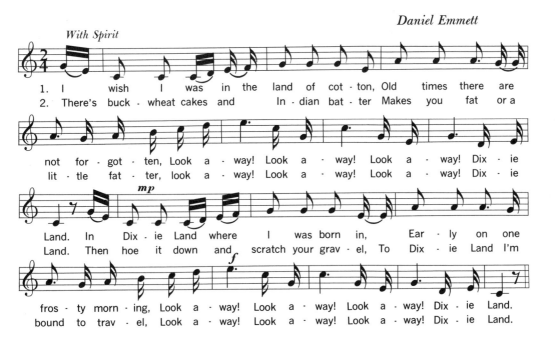

With Spirit

1. I wish I was in the land of cot - ton, Old times there are
2. There's buck - wheat cakes and In - dian bat - ter Makes you fat or a

not for - got - ten, Look a - way! Look a - way! Look a - way! Dix - ie
lit - tle fat - ter, look a - way! Look a - way! Look a - way! Dix - ie

mp

Land. In Dix - ie Land where I was born in, Ear - ly on one
Land. Then hoe it down and scratch your grav - el, To Dix - ie Land I'm

f

fros - ty morn - ing, Look a - way! Look a - way! Look a - way! Dix - ie Land.
bound to trav - el, Look a - way! Look a - way! Look a - way! Dix - ie Land.

23

Refrain

Then I wish I was in Dix - ie, Hoo - ray! Hoo - ray! In _____

Dix - ie Land I'll take my stand, To live and die in Dix - ie, A -

way, A - way, A - way down south in Dix - ie, A -

way, A - way, A - way down south in Dix - ie.

EVENING SONG*

Carl Maria von Weber

Soft - ly sighs the breath of eve - ning, Steal - ing through the shadow - y grove,

While the stars in hea - ven shin - ing Keep their si - lent watch a - bove.

Syncopation

A device used to add zest and interest to rhythm is the shifting of accent from the strong beat to a normally weaker beat. In other words, the accent is changed from an expected to an unexpected place. For example, in a grouping of four beats, the emphasis or stress is on the second or fourth beat rather than on the first and third; in a grouping of three beats, it is on the second or third rather than on the first. This "offbeat" rhythm is known as syncopation. It is used extensively in jazz, but it is also found in folk music and in compositions by many famous composers, such as Beethoven, Schumann, and Brahms.

Syncopated rhythm   *Regular or smooth rhythm*

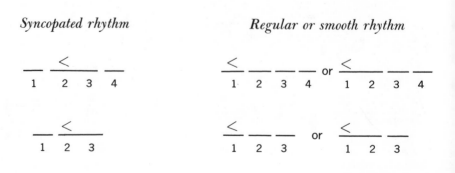

examples

LI'L 'LIZA JANE

American Song

1. There's a gal in Bal-ti-more, Li'l 'Li-za Jane, She's the one that I a-dore, Li'l 'Li-za Jane.
2. I got a house in Bal-ti-more, Li'l 'Li-za Jane, Brus-sels car-pet on my floor, Li'l 'Li-za Jane.

Refrain

Oh! E-li-za, Li'l 'Li-za Jane; Oh! E-li-za, Li'l 'Li-za Jane.

3. I got a house in Baltimore, Li'l 'Liza Jane,
    Silver doorplate on my door, Li'l 'Liza Jane.

4. Come, my love, and marry me, Li'l 'Liza Jane,
    And I'll take good care of thee, Li'l 'Liza Jane.

Syncopated rhythm

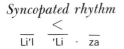

Li'l 'Li - za

Regular or smooth rhythm

Li'l 'Li - za

COCKLES AND MUSSELS*

Old Irish Song

Lively

In Dub-lin's fair cit-y, where girls are so pret-ty,'Twas there I first met with sweet

Mol-ly Ma-lone; She drove a wheel-bar-row through streets broad and nar-row, Sing-ing

Refrain

"Cock-les and mus-sels, a-live, all a-live!" A-live, a-live oh!___ a-live, a-live

Fine Slower

oh! ___ Sing-ing "Cock-les and mus-sels a-live, all a-live!" She died of the "fa-ver," and

noth-ing could save her, And that was the end of sweet Mol-ly Ma-lone; But her ghost drives a

D.S. al Fine

bar-row through streets broad and nar-row, Sing-ing "Cock-les and mus-sels a-live, all a-live!

MY LORD, WHAT A MORNING

Moderato

Negro Spiritual

My Lord, what a morn - ing, My Lord, what a morn - ing,

My Lord, what a morn - ing, When the stars be - gin to fall.

Fine

1. You'll hear the trum - pet sound To wake the na - tions un - der ground,
2. You'll hear the sin - ner mourn To wake the na - tions un - der ground,

D.S. al Fine

Look - ing at my God's right hand When the stars be - gin to fall.
Look - ing at my God's right hand When the stars be - gin to fall.

THE QUILTING PARTY

College Song

In the sky the bright stars glit - tered, ___ On the bank the pale moon shone,

And 'twas from Aunt Di - nah's quilt - ing par - ty I was see - ing Nel - lie home.

Fine

I was see - ing Nel - lie home, ___ I was see - ing Nel - lie home.

D.S. al Fine

ROBIN ADAIR

Caroline Keppel

Scotch Air

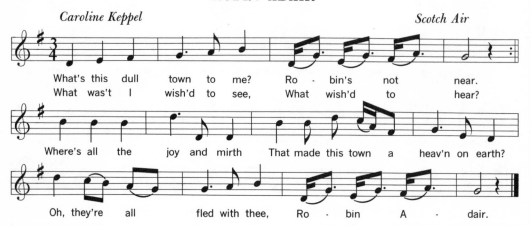

What's this dull town to me? Ro - bin's not near.
What was't I wish'd to see, What wish'd to hear?

Where's all the joy and mirth That made this town a heav'n on earth?

Oh, they're all fled with thee, Ro - bin A - dair.

Assignment

1. Draw line pictures of the pitch and rhythm patterns of "Now the Day Is Over" (page 5), "Joy to the World" (page 5), and "America" (page 12).

2. Can you recognize some of the songs you have sung, such as "America," "The Star-Spangled Banner," and "Oh, Susanna," when you hear their melodic rhythm tapped or clapped? Try this with some familiar songs which have distinctive rhythm to see if your classmates recognize them.

3. After hearing and singing the following songs, decide how they are grouped, whether in beats of 1 2, 1 2 3, 1 2 3 4, or 1 2 3 4 5 6. Show how you feel this grouping by clapping, by tapping, and by moving your hand and arm as a conductor does.

EVENTIDE

Ludwig van Beethoven
(Theme from Ninth Symphony)

LULLABY

Scotch Folk Song

SILENT NIGHT

Joseph Mohr   *Franz Gruber*

MARCHING SONG

Arranged from Wagner

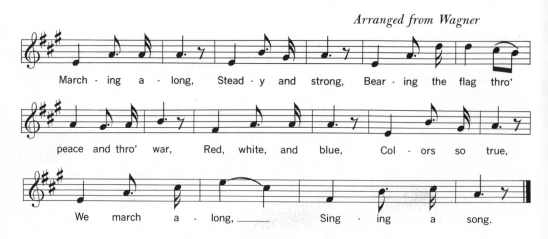

4. Find six examples of songs other than those mentioned in this chapter to illustrate the expressiveness of rhythm.

5. **a** What is meant by "syncopation"?

    b In the songs given in this chapter to illustrate syncopation, point out just where syncopation occurs. Show the relation of the melody to the basic beats by drawing lines and by clapping, tapping, and moving your hand and arm as you sing.

6. Sing the syncopated parts of each song in regular or smooth rhythm and then in syncopation to demonstrate how syncopation affects the character of the music.

7. Has syncopation occurred in any songs you have sung in preceding chapters? If so, in which ones? Indicate specifically where syncopation is found.

The Staff

As music developed as an art, a means of recording it definitely and permanently became increasingly necessary. Finally, after several centuries, five parallel, equidistant lines, called the "staff," came into use. The staff, however, is not restricted to these five lines and the four spaces between them. It can be extended either up or down by means of short lines known as "ledger lines."

Degree Names

Each line and space, called a "degree," is numbered from the lower to the higher as follows: first line, second line, third line, fourth line, and fifth line; first space, second space, third space, and fourth space; first ledger line below the staff, first ledger line above the staff, and so forth.

The degree names of the staff are the first seven letters of the alphabet: A, B, C, D, E, F, G. The exact location of these, however, is not determined until a clef (from the Latin word *clavis,* meaning "key") is placed at the beginning of the staff in such a manner as to indicate one degree. From this, the others are readily determined.

Clef Signs

G, or treble, staff

F, or bass, staff

The G clef (a form of the old Gothic G), which encircles the second line of the upper, or treble, staff, indicates that this line is G. The F clef (derived from the old Gothic F), which originates on the fourth line of the bass staff, indicates that this line is F. The G, or treble, staff is used for higher-pitched voices and instruments and for the right hand in playing the piano. Conversely, the F, or bass, staff is for lower-pitched voices and instruments and for the left hand in playing the piano. Together, the G and F staffs form the great, or grand, staff.

musical notation

4

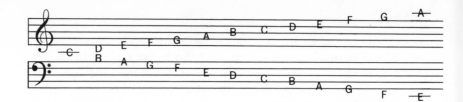

Bar, or Measure, Lines

Even a casual glance at printed music shows you that the staff is marked off in regular spaces by vertical lines; these are called "bars." The space between two bar lines is a "measure"—a unit of rhythm. A double bar marks the end of a composition or a section of it.

Notes and Rests

On the staff are symbols known as notes and rests. Notes represent pitches of tones and their relative duration. The higher the pitch, the higher is the placement of notes on the staff, and vice versa. Silence in music is indicated by rests, which consume the same length of time as the corresponding note (whole note, whole rest; half note, half rest; etc.). Notes and rests commonly found in elementary school music books are:

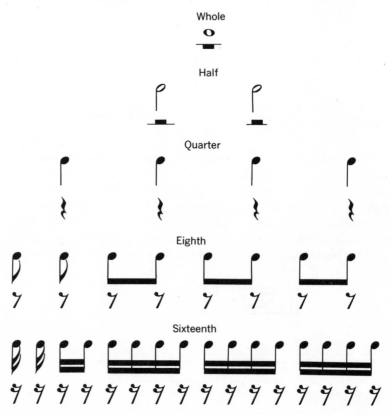

30

dotted notes and rests

A dot placed after a note or rest increases its value by one-half.

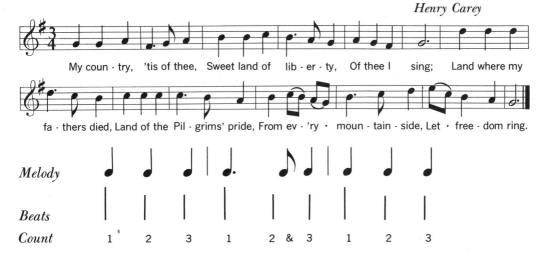

You will encounter dotted notes frequently, for they create a distinctive, interesting quality to music. Notice the effect of the dot and its relation to the beat in the following songs.

AMERICA

Henry Carey

My coun - try, 'tis of thee, Sweet land of lib - er - ty, Of thee I sing; Land where my

fa - thers died, Land of the Pil - grims' pride, From ev - 'ry · moun - tain - side, Let · free - dom ring.

Melody

Beats

Count   1   2   3   1   2 & 3   1   2   3

WE GATHER TOGETHER*

Traditional Dutch Tune

1. We gath - er to - geth - er to ask the Lord's bless - ing; He chas - tens and has - tens His
2. Be - side us to guide us, our God with us join - ing, Or - dain - ing, main - tain - ing His

will to make known. The wick - ed op - press - ing, now cease ____ from dis -
king - dom di - vine. So from the be - gin - ning, the fight ____ we were

tress - ing. Sing prais - es to His name; He for - gets not His own.
win - ning. Thou, Lord, wast at our side; ____ all glo - ry be Thine.

31

BATTLE HYMN OF THE REPUBLIC*

Julia Ward Howe

William Steffe

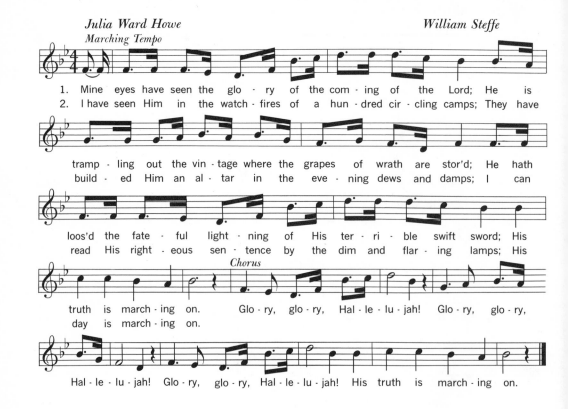

1. Mine eyes have seen the glo - ry of the com - ing of the Lord; He is
2. I have seen Him in the watch - fires of a hun - dred cir - cling camps; They have

tramp - ling out the vin - tage where the grapes of wrath are stor'd; He hath
build - ed Him an al - tar in the eve - ning dews and damps; I can

loos'd the fate - ful light - ning of His ter - ri - ble swift sword; His
read His right - eous sen - tence by the dim and flar - ing lamps; His

Chorus

truth is march - ing on. Glo - ry, glo - ry, Hal - le - lu - jah! Glo - ry, glo - ry,
day is march - ing on.

Hal - le - lu - jah! Glo - ry, glo - ry, Hal - le - lu - jah! His truth is march - ing on.

AWAY IN A MANGER

Martin Luther

Carl Mueller

32

1. A - way in a man - ger, No crib for his bed, The lit - tle Lord Je - sus Laid
2. The cat - tle are low - ing, The poor Babe a - wakes, But lit - tle Lord Je - sus No

down His sweet head; The stars in the sky Look'd down where he
cry - ing He makes; I love Thee, Lord Je - sus, Look down from the

lay, The lit - tle Lord Je - sus A - sleep on the hay.
sky, And stay by my cra - dle 'Till morn - ing is nigh.

WEEL MAY THE KEEL ROW

Scotch Folk Song

1. As I went up to Sand-gate, to Sand-gate, to Sand-gate, As I went
2. Weel ___ may the keel row, the keel row, the keel ___ row, Weel ___

up to Sand-gate, I heard a las-sie sing. Oh, weel ___ may the keel row, the
may the keel row That my ___ lad-die's in.

Fine Refrain

D.C. al Fine

keel row, the keel ___ row, Oh, weel ___ may the keel row That my ___ lad-die's in.

The Tie

An arched line connecting successive notes of the same pitch, called a "tie" (⌣), indicates that these notes have one continuous sound with a total value equal to the untied notes. Specifically, if a half note is tied to a quarter note (♩ ♩), the tone would be equal in duration to a dotted half note; two quarter notes tied (♩ ♩) would be equal to a half note.

The tie should not be confused with the slur, which unites notes on different degrees of the staff and means that two or more pitches are to be sung to one syllable of a word or to a word of one syllable.

You can see and hear the difference between the tie and the slur in the song "When Johnny Comes Marching Home."

WHEN JOHNNY COMES MARCHING HOME*

Louis Lambert

With Spirit

1. When John-ny comes march-ing home a-gain, Hur-rah, hur-rah! We'll
2. Get read-y for the Ju-bi-lee, Hur-rah, hur-rah! We'll

give him a heart-y wel-come then, Hur-rah, hur-rah! The
give the he-ro three times three, Hur-rah, hur-rah! The

33

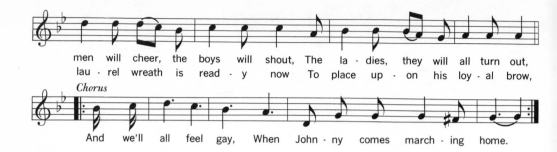

men will cheer, the boys will shout, The la - dies, they will all turn out,
lau - rel wreath is read - y now To place up - on his loy - al brow,

Chorus

And we'll all feel gay, When John - ny comes march - ing home.

Triplets

Three notes grouped together by a curved line with the number 3 placed under or above it are known as a "triplet." These notes are to be performed in the time given to two of the same value. See, for example, "Row, Row, Row Your Boat" (page 6) and "Dixie" (page 23).

Sharps and Flats

Modification of pitch is shown by the use of sharps (♯) and flats (♭). A sharp raises a tone by a semitone, and a flat lowers it by a semitone.[1] The natural (♮) cancels a previous sharp or flat. Notice the placement and the effect of these in the following songs.[2]

GOOD-BYE[3]

Tosti

p

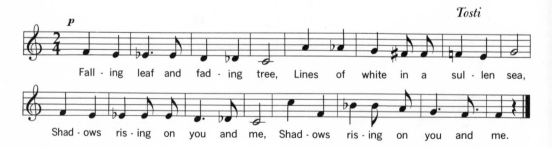

Fall - ing leaf and fad - ing tree, Lines of white in a sul - len sea,

Shad - ows ris - ing on you and me, Shad - ows ris - ing on you and me.

34

1. A tone can be raised two semitones or a whole tone by the use of the symbol 𝄪 (a double sharp). It can be lowered two semitones or a whole tone by the use of the symbol ♭♭ (a double flat). These occur infrequently in elementary school songs.

2. Note to the teacher: Play these songs with and without the chromatic alterations to show students just how they affect the melody.

3. Excerpt.

SWEET AND LOW*

Alfred Tennyson

Joseph Barnby

Slowly and Smoothly

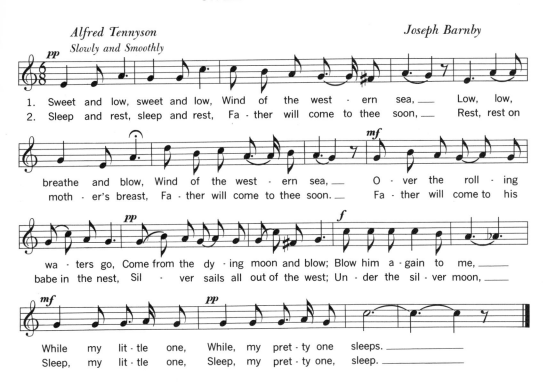

1. Sweet and low, sweet and low, Wind of the west - ern sea, — Low, low,
2. Sleep and rest, sleep and rest, Fa - ther will come to thee soon, — Rest, rest on

breathe and blow, Wind of the west - ern sea, — O - ver the roll - ing
moth - er's breast, Fa - ther will come to thee soon. — Fa - ther will come to his

wa - ters go, Come from the dy - ing moon and blow; Blow him a - gain to me, —
babe in the nest, Sil - ver sails all out of the west; Un - der the sil - ver moon, —

While my lit - tle one, While, my pret - ty one sleeps. —
Sleep, my lit - tle one, Sleep, my pret - ty one, sleep. —

SANTA LUCIA*

Neapolitan Folk Song

Moderately

1. Now 'neath the sil - ver moon o - cean is glow - ing, O'er the calm bil - low
   Here balm - y breez - es blow, pure joys in - vite us, And as we gent - ly row,
2. When o'er thy wa - ters light winds are play - ing, Thy spell can sooth us,
   To thee, sweet Na - po - li, what charms are giv - en, Where smiles cre - a - tion,

Refrain

soft winds are blow - ing; Hark, how the sail - or's cry Joy - ous - ly
all things de - light us. Home of fair Po - e - sy, Realm of pure
all care al - lay - ing;
toil blest by heav - en.

ech - oes nigh: San - ta Lu - ci - a! San - ta Lu - ci - a!
Har - mo - ny, San - ta Lu - ci - a! San - ta Lu - ci - a!

35

Assignment

1. Name the staff degree on which each note is placed.

(C)

(C)

2. Place the following in the proper places on both the G (treble) and the F (bass) staffs.

Example   C G

D Eb G Bb G# B C# E Gb F A

Db Ab C A# F#

3. Practice singing with the degree names the following songs:
    "May Day Carol" (page 7)
    "Vesper Hymn" (page 7)
    "O Rest in the Lord" (page 10)
    "Old Folks at Home" (page 12)
    "Wait for the Wagon" (page 19)

4. Clap or tap the basic beats as you sing the songs illustrating the use of the dot (pages 31 to 33).

5. Find five songs in preceding chapters where the dot is used *within* the song.

6. Show the relationship of the dot to the beat by making line pictures of the melody and the beats in four songs. (See illustration, page 31.)

7. What is the difference between the tie and the slur? Find four songs in preceding chapters that illustrate the use of the tie and four that illustrate the use of the slur.

8. Explain the following and find specific examples in songs:

♯,   ♭,   ♮,   ⌐1￢ ,   ⌐2￣

9. It is important that you learn to make musical symbols quickly and accurately. For practice, copy "Sweet and Low" (page 35) and "Santa Lucia" (page 35).[4]

---

4. See Appendix C (page 161) for directions on how to write musical notation.

Meter Signatures

You have already learned that the rhythm or movement of music groups into accents, or beats. The notation of music shows you exactly what this grouping is by the use of bars which separate the music into measures. Near the beginning of the staff are two numbers, one placed above the other. These are the meter signatures, sometimes called "time signatures." The upper number indicates the number of beats in a measure, and the lower number is the unit of measurement, or the kind of note that is to receive one beat. The signature $\frac{2}{4}$, for example, shows you that there are two beats in a measure, with the quarter note (or its equivalent) getting one beat ($\frac{2}{4}$). Likewise, the sign $\frac{3}{8}$ at the beginning of the music means that the measures have three beats, with each eighth note (or its equivalent) receiving one beat ($\frac{3}{8}$), and so forth.

Meter signatures that you will find frequently are $\frac{2}{2}$, $\frac{2}{4}$, $\frac{3}{4}$, $\frac{3}{8}$, $\frac{4}{4}$, $\frac{6}{8}$, C, and ¢. The signature $\frac{4}{4}$ is also known as "common time." It is often indicated by the sign C.[1]

A line through C (¢) indicates duple meter in quick time, with a half note receiving one beat ($\frac{2}{2}$). It is sometimes referred to as "cut time" or "alla breve" (from the Italian, meaning "according to the breve or note"). See, for example, "She'll Be Coming 'Round the Mountain" (page 15).

Some songs in $\frac{6}{8}$ meter have a basic beat of six, with each eighth note getting one beat, as "Drink to Me Only with Thine Eyes" (page 9). But there are songs with this signature that are to be sung in quick tempo, two beats to a measure, the dotted quarter note getting one beat ($\frac{2}{2}$). The rate of speed at which you sing some songs and their basic character may also change the beat pattern of other measure groupings. For instance, some songs marked $\frac{4}{4}$ are in beats of two to a measure, and some marked $\frac{3}{4}$ swing in beats of one to a measure.

two beats to a measure

SKIP TO MY LOU

Singing Game

Lost my part - ner, what'll I do? Lost my part - ner,
what'll I do? Lost my part - ner, what'll I do?
Skip to my Lou, my dar - ling.

---

1. The sign C is a survival of the old mensural system of notation, in which the perfect circle was used for perfect, or triple, time and the broken circle (C) represented the imperfect, or duple, plan.

two beats to a measure

SAILING

Godfrey Marks

Sail - ing, sail - ing o - ver the bound - ing main;

For man - y a storm - y wind shall blow ere Jack comes home a - gain.

Sail - ing, sail - ing o - ver the bound - ing main;

For man - y a storm - y wind shall blow ere Jack comes home a - gain.

two beats to a measure

GOOD KING WENCESLAS

Traditional Carol

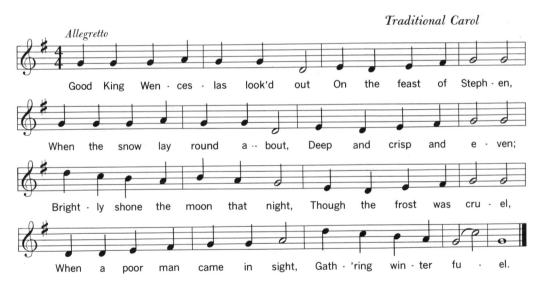

Allegretto

Good King Wen - ces - las look'd out On the feast of Steph - en,

When the snow lay round a - bout, Deep and crisp and e - ven;

Bright - ly shone the moon that night, Though the frost was cru - el,

When a poor man came in sight, Gath - 'ring win - ter fu - el.

one beat to a measure

39

SKATER'S SONG

Emil Waldteufel

We glide a - long, ___ Sing - ing a song, ___ Skat - ers a - way, We glide and sway. ___

Incomplete Measures

Although there can be a greater or fewer number of notes in a measure than the time signature indicates, the total value of the notes can be neither more nor less than the signature shows. Many songs, however, begin on part of the last measure. For example, if a song with $\frac{4}{4}$ signature begins on a quarter note, or the last beat of a measure, the last measure of the song has a note or notes equal only to three quarter notes, or three beats.

First measure	Last measure
4th beat	1st, 2d, 3d beats

Among songs beginning on the last beat of a measure are "The Blue Bells of Scotland" (page 6), "May Day Carol" (page 7), "The Little Sandman" (page 14), "Flow Gently, Sweet Afton" (page 16), and "The Star-Spangled Banner" (page 22).

Change of Signatures within a Song

Basic beats within the measures are usually but not always maintained throughout a song. Sometimes, to give variety and expressiveness and to keep the rhythm of the words, the measure beat changes. Hence you will find songs with some measures in $\frac{4}{4}$ meter followed by some in $\frac{3}{4}$, some in $\frac{6}{8}$ followed by some in $\frac{4}{4}$, and so forth.

SHENANDOAH

Sea Chantey

1. Oh, Shen - an - doah, I long to hear you, Oh, Shen -
2. Oh, Shen - an - doah, I love your daugh - ter, Way, · hey! You roll - ing riv - er! 'Tis sev'n
3. Oh, Shen - an - doah, I love her dear - ly, I'll work

an - doah, I long to hear you.
long years since last I saw her. Way, hey! We're bound a - way, 'Cross the wide Mis - sou - ri.
for her and pay you dear - ly.

HERE WE COME A-WASSAILING*

Traditional

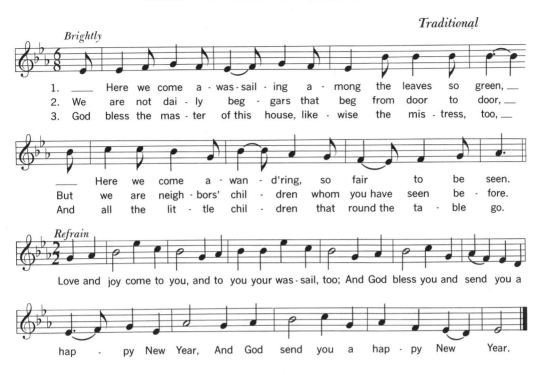

Brightly

1. ___ Here we come a-wassailing a-mong the leaves so green, ___
2. We are not dai-ly beg-gars that beg from door to door, ___
3. God bless the mas-ter of this house, like-wise the mis-tress, too, ___

___ Here we come a-wan-d'ring, so fair to be seen.
But we are neigh-bors' chil-dren whom you have seen be-fore.
And all the lit-tle chil-dren that round the ta-ble go.

Refrain

Love and joy come to you, and to you your was-sail, too; And God bless you and send you a

hap - py New Year, And God send you a hap-py New Year.

THE BARNYARD SONG

Kentucky Mountain Folk Song

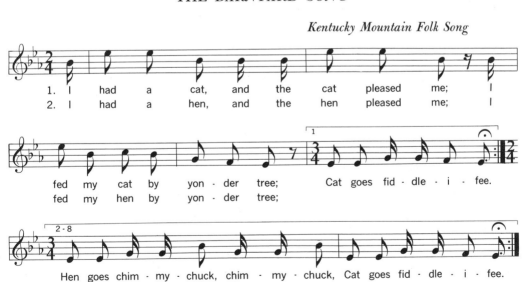

1. I had a cat, and the cat pleased me; I
2. I had a hen, and the hen pleased me; I

fed my cat by yon-der tree; Cat goes fid-dle-i-fee.
fed my hen by yon-der tree;

Hen goes chim-my-chuck, chim-my-chuck, Cat goes fid-dle-i-fee.

3. Duck goes quack, quack,
4. Goose goes sssss, sssss,
5. Sheep goes baa, baa,

6. Pig goes oinck, oinck,
7. Cow goes moo, moo,
8. Horse goes neigh, neigh,

41

THE TWELVE DAYS OF CHRISTMAS*2

Old English Folk Song

On the first day of Christ-mas, my true love sent to me A par-tridge___ in a pear tree.

2. On the sec-ond day of Christ-mas, my true love sent to me
3. On the third ___ day of Christ-mas, my true love sent to me
4. On the fourth ___ day of Christ-mas, my true love sent to me

Two tur-tle doves, And a par-tridge ___ in a pear tree.
Three French ___ hens,
Four col-ly birds,

5. On the fifth day of Christ-mas, my true love sent to me Five gol-den rings,

Four ___ col-ly birds, Three French hens, Two ___ tur-tle doves, and a par-tridge___ in a pear tree.

6. On the sixth day of Christ-mas, my true love sent to me
7. On the seventh day of Christ-mas, my true love sent to me

Six geese a-lay-ing, Five gol-den rings, Four ___ col-ly birds,
Seven swans a-swim-ming,

Three French hens, Two ___ tur-tle doves, and a par-tridge ___ in a pear tree.

8. On the eighth day . . .
   Eight maids a-milking, . . .
9. On the ninth day . . .
   Nine ladies dancing, . . .
10. On the tenth day . . .
    Ten lords a-leaping, . . .
11. On the eleventh day . . .
    Eleven pipers piping, . . .

12. On the twelfth day of Christmas,
    My true love sent to me
    Twelve drummers drumming, Eleven pipers piping,
    Ten lords a-leaping, Nine ladies dancing,
    Eight maids a-milking, Seven swans a-swimming,
    Six geese a-laying, Five golden rings,
    Four colly birds, Three French hens,
    Two turtle doves, and a partridge in a pear tree.

Melody used by permission of Novello & Co., Ltd., London.

2. As each item is added in successive verses, the preceding items are repeated in reverse order.

Assignment

1. What is meant by the "meter" of music?
2. Indicate the correct meter signatures in the following:

3. Where should the measure bars be placed?

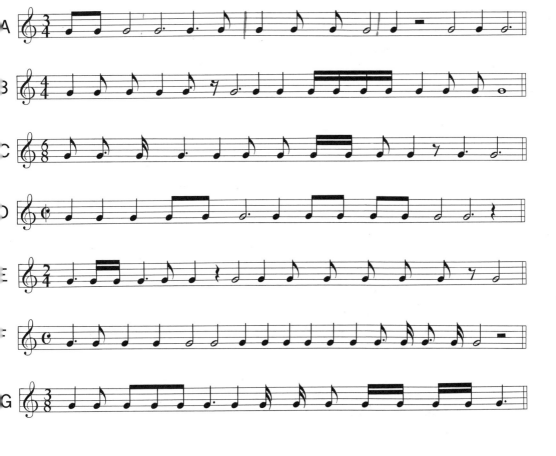

43

4. The instructor should divide the class into three groups: one group to chant the melodic rhythm with the sound *ta* on a pitch comfortable for all, the second group to indicate the basic measure beats by hitting rhythm sticks or by counting, and the third group to mark the strong beats by tapping drums or by clapping.

Example

Chant

Rhythm sticks or count

Drums or clap

six beats to a measure

two beats to a measure in the 6/8 *exercise*

44

5. Create your own rhythmic patterns by writing four measures in 2/4, 3/4, 4/4, and 6/8 meter. Use different notes and rests and include at least one syncopated measure in each.

6. Complete the last measure of the following:

7. Conduct the songs listed on page 40 that do not begin on the first beat of the measure. See directions in Appendix A (page 159).

8. Select four other familiar songs that do not begin on the first beat of the measure to conduct for the class to sing.

9. As you sing songs where the meter changes within the song (pages 40 to 42), clap the basic beats or tap them on a drum or tap rhythm sticks. Conduct the songs with the baton movements.

Wind Instruments

Learning to play instruments is an effective way to further your skills in the use of musical notation. Among the simple, easy-to-play wind instruments are the tonette, song flute, and flutophone. These, however, are limited in range and musical possibilities. More satisfactory is the recorder, a member of the flute family which was widely used during the fifteenth to eighteenth centuries. Interest in it was revived about 1920. It has a pleasing, musical tone with accurate intonation and presents few technical difficulties to the beginning pupil. It comes in different sizes: soprano, alto, tenor, and bass. The first three have a full two-octave chromatic range; the bass recorder has a smaller range and is used mainly in ensembles. A fifth recorder, the sopranino, is seldom used.[1]

Percussion Melodic Instruments

Since you cannot play a wind instrument and sing at the same time, the percussion melodic instruments constructed for classroom use are better adapted for a singing class. These are bars of graduated lengths set in horizontal frames and are sounded by striking with mallets. Some of the bars are made of wood, as in xylophones; others are made of metal, as in bells. Since metal bars have a more penetrating, resonant sound than do those made of wood, they are recommended for this course.

Tuned resonator bells are separate tone bars. These can be handed to different individuals in a class to play one tone as directed, or the bars can be assembled and played as a single instrument by one person. Two sets are available, an eight-bar instrument with a range from middle C to the C an octave above, and a twenty-bell set which plays chromatically from middle C to G above the staff. Song, or melody, bells are also available in different sizes, ranging from one to two and one-half octaves. The larger chromatic instruments are more useful than the smaller ones.

When playing the song bells, hold the mallet firmly in your hand and keep your wrist flexible so that after you strike a bar it can rebound quickly and be ready for the next tone. Names of the bars of the song bells are the same as those of the staff degrees (A, B, C, D, etc.) and are stamped into the metal. Therefore, if you have learned to recognize and name the staff degrees quickly and accurately, you will find it easy to play songs on the bells.

Assignment

1. Strike the bars of the song bells in different places to determine just where you get the best quality of tone.

2. Play the following, beginning with middle C:

C E G; Ab C Eb; D F# A; F A C; E G# B
Bb Db F; C# E G#; F# A C#; G Bb D; C Eb G

1. If you wish to experiment with these instruments, you can obtain them from any instrument dealer. The cost is minimal. See Appendix F (page 168) for a list of instruction books which give complete directions for playing.

classroom melodic instruments

6

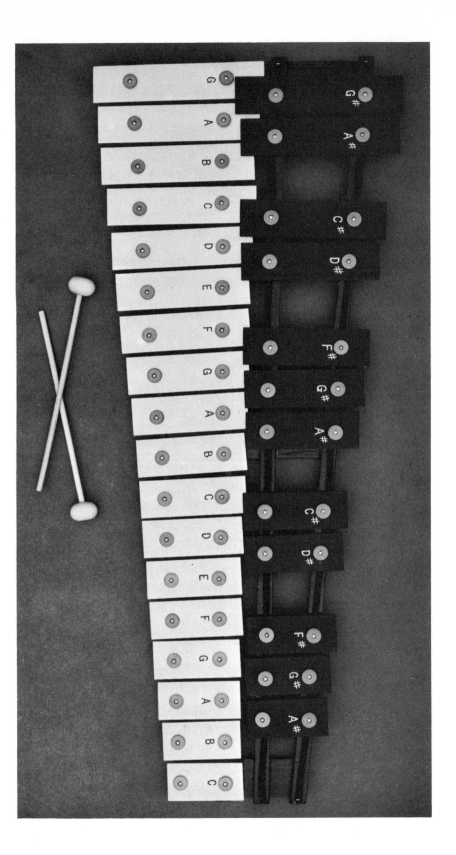

47

3. Play:

4. Select four familiar songs from the preceding chapters to play on the song bells.

5. Play, then sing, "White Coral Bells," "My Pony," and "The Little Girl and the Robin." Select a portion of each song to play as an introduction and as a coda (ending) to the song.

WHITE CORAL BELLS

Traditional

1. White cor - al bells up - on a slen - der stalk,
2. Oh, don't you wish that you could hear them ring?

Lil - ies of the val - ley deck my gar - den walk.
That will hap - pen on - ly when the fair - ies sing.

MY PONY

German Folk Song

Trot, trot, trot! Go, and nev - er stop! Where it's smooth and where it's ston - y,

Trot a - long, my lit - tle po - ny; Go, and nev - er stop! Trot, trot, trot, trot, trot!

48

THE LITTLE GIRL AND THE ROBIN

Traditional

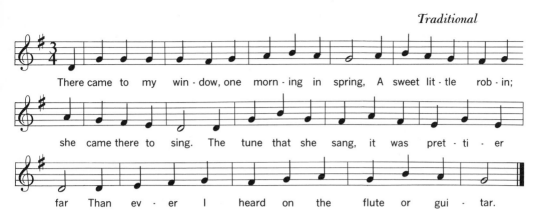

There came to my win-dow, one morn-ing in spring, A sweet lit-tle rob-in;

she came there to sing. The tune that she sang, it was pret-ti-er

far Than ev-er I heard on the flute or gui-tar.

49

The piano was invented early in the eighteenth century by Bartolommeo Cristofori, a harpsichord maker from Italy. In 1709, he replaced the quills which plucked the strings of the harpsichord with hammers which hit the strings. This ensured a fuller, more resonant tone. Cristofori called his instrument *gravicembali col piano e forte* ("harpsichord with soft and loud") to indicate that it could more effectively produce changes in dynamics than the regular harpsichord. The name later was changed to *pianoforte* and then to *piano*.

Although the perfection of the piano was gradual, by 1860 it had practically all of the elements of the modern instrument. Twentieth-century pianos in common use are the concert grand, the baby or parlor grand, and the upright. The large upright has been replaced with a smaller-sized one known as the "spinet."

The piano is frequently called "the universal instrument" because it is adapted both to the amateur and the professional musician, the child and the adult. Although it takes years of study to play it well, you will discover in the following pages that in a relatively few hours of thoughtful practice, you can become proficient enough to make the piano an instrument of usefulness and pleasure.

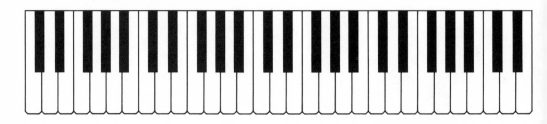

The Piano Keyboard

When studied in connection with the staff, the piano keyboard gives a clear representation of the relationship of pitches. If you observe the plan carefully, you will notice a regular pattern formed by the black and white keys. The black keys are grouped in twos and threes and alternate with the white keys except in two places. This pattern is repeated over and over throughout the range of the instrument. In each single grouping of black and white keys, there are twelve different tones, those made by five black and seven white keys. From a white key to its nearest neighbor is one half step. The distance from one white key to the next white key when a black key intervenes is one whole step.

Names of the Piano Keys

The close relationship that exists between the staff and the piano keyboard is indicated by the fact that the first seven letters of the alphabet are also used to name the piano keys. The white key to the left of the two black keys is C. To its right, the other white keys are, successively, D, E, F, G, A, B, and then C again. From C to C, counting only the white keys, are eight tones, or an octave, as from D to D, E to E, F to F, and so forth. Near the middle of the piano keyboard (near the nameplate) is "middle C." This is an important key for you to locate and remember because it serves as a guide to the other keys.

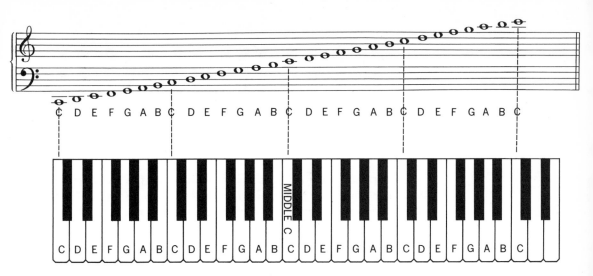

The black keys are named from their neighboring white keys thus: When the black key between C and D is associated with and named from the white key to its left, it is called "C sharp"—the term "sharp" and its symbol (♯) meaning "one half step higher." When the same black key is named from its neighbor to the right, it is called "D flat"—the term "flat" and its symbol (♭) meaning "one half step lower." In other words, in the ascending order of keys, the black key is named from the white key to its left, with the word "sharp" added; and in the descending order of keys, the black key is named from the white key to its right, with the word "flat" added.

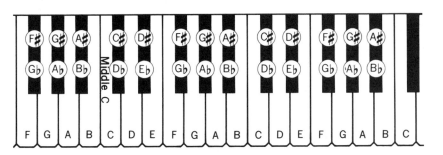

Playing the Piano

When playing the piano, sit erect, facing the instrument approximately at its center. Do not be concerned with the pedals[1] until you are thoroughly familiar with the keyboard and can finger it easily. Therefore, keep both feet on the floor. Place your hands in a curved position so that you can press the keys naturally and effectively. As an aid, number your fingers 1, 2, 3, 4, 5, counting the thumb as 1. The right hand plays the treble staff; the left hand plays the bass.

1. See Appendix B (page 160) for a discussion of the piano pedals.

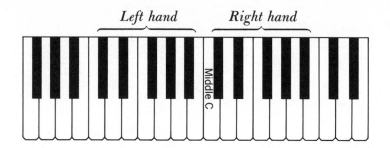

Left hand   *Right hand*

Middle C

When you need a wider playing range than your five fingers provide, pass the thumb under your fingers and your fingers over your thumb. For example, when playing a sequence of eight white keys in ascending order beginning with C, place the thumb of your right hand on C and then pass it under your third finger to play the fourth tone. Starting with the little, or fifth, finger of your left hand, pass the third finger over your thumb for the sixth tone, or A. In the descending order, begin with the little, or fifth, finger of your right hand and pass the third finger over your thumb for the sixth tone, or E; begin with the thumb of your left hand on C and pass it under the third finger to strike G.

Right hand

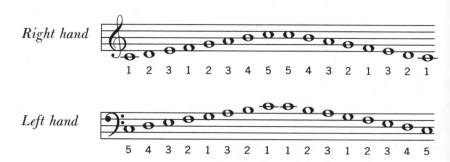

1 2 3 1 2 3 4 5 5 4 3 2 1 3 2 1

Left hand

5 4 3 2 1 3 2 1 1 2 3 1 2 3 4 5

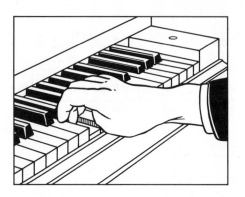

Assignment

1. Describe the plan of the piano keyboard and tell how the keys are named.

2. Find and play the various keys on the piano or the keyboard chart as your instructor dictates, such as "Find all the C's, the E's, the G's," and so forth.

3. Name and play the following on the piano or the keyboard chart:

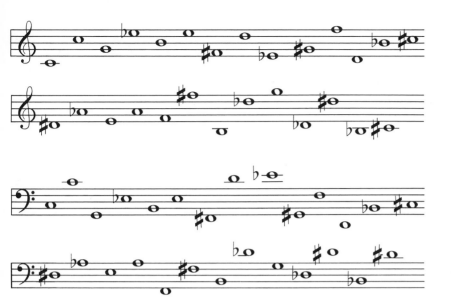

4. Practice the fingering for playing the eight white keys beginning and ending on C, as given on page 52. Use the same fingering beginning and ending on D, E, etc., ignoring the black keys.

5. Play the following exercises using the fingering indicated:

53

6. Sing the following melodies before you attempt to play them. You may be more successful if you play the melody first (the right hand) and then the notes for the left hand before using them together.

YANKEE DOODLE

Unknown

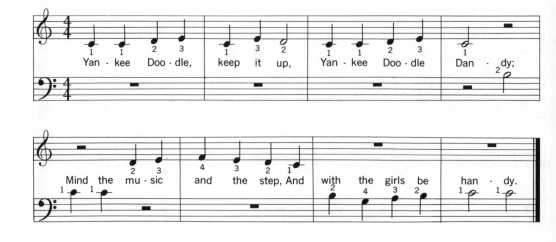

Yan - kee Doo - dle, keep it up, Yan - kee Doo - dle Dan - dy;

Mind the mu - sic and the step, And with the girls be han - dy.

54

HOT CROSS BUNS

Traditional

Hot cross buns, Hot cross buns, One a pen - ny, two a pen - ny, Hot cross buns.

ARE YOU SLEEPING, BROTHER JOHN?

French Round

Are you sleep - ing, Are you sleep - ing, Broth - er John, Broth - er John?

Morn - ing bells are ring - ing, Morn - ing bells are ring - ing, Ding, dang, dong! Ding, dang, dong!

OLD MACDONALD HAD A FARM

Traditional

Fine

Old Mac - Don - ald had a farm, E - I - E - I - O!

And on this farm he had some chicks, E - I - E - I - O!

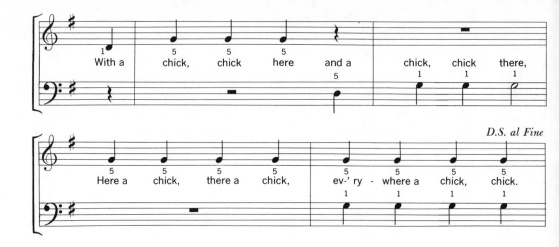

D.S. al Fine

AT PIERROT'S DOOR

French Folk Song

56

MARY HAD A LITTLE LAMB

Traditional

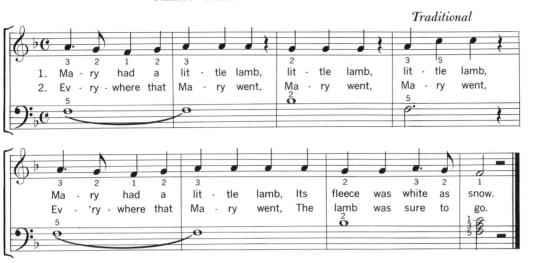

LIGHTLY ROW

German Folk Tune

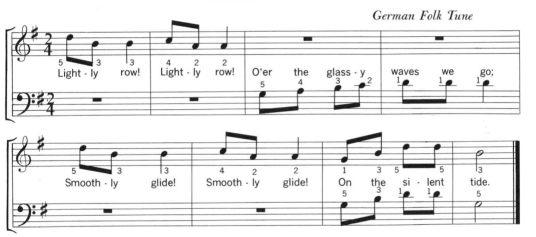

GOOD KING WENCESLAS

Traditional Carol

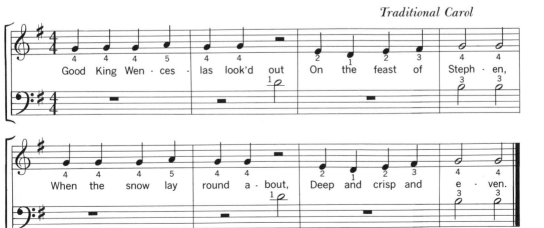

57

POLLY, PUT THE KETTLE ON

English Nursery Rhyme

1. Pol - ly, put the ket - tle on; Pol - ly, put the ket - tle on;
2. Slice the bread and but - ter fine; Slice the bread and but - ter fine;

Pol - ly, put the ket - tle on, We'll all have tea.
Slice e - nough for eight or nine, We'll all have tea.

LONDON BRIDGE

Singing Game

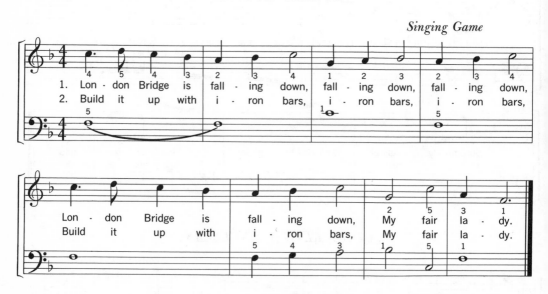

1. Lon - don Bridge is fall - ing down, fall - ing down, fall - ing down,
2. Build it up with i - ron bars, i - ron bars, i - ron bars,

Lon - don Bridge is fall - ing down, My fair la - dy.
Build it up with i - ron bars, My fair la - dy.

CRADLE SONG

J. Rousseau

Hush, my babe, lie still and slum - ber; Ho - ly an - gels guard thy bed.

SLEEP, BABY, SLEEP

German Folk Song

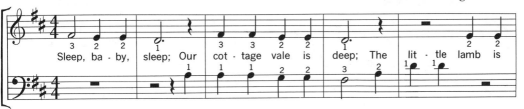

Sleep, ba - by, sleep; Our cot - tage vale is deep; The lit - tle lamb is

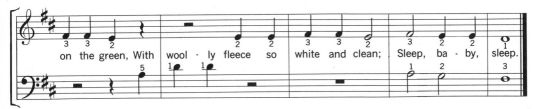

on the green, With wool - ly fleece so white and clean; Sleep, ba - by, sleep.

OH WHERE HAS MY LITTLE DOG GONE?

Traditional

Oh where, oh where has my lit - tle dog gone? Oh where, oh where can he be?

With his ears cut short and his tail cut long, Oh where, oh where can he be?

MERRILY WE ROLL ALONG

Old Song

Mer - ri - ly we roll a - long, Roll a - long, roll a - long,

59

Mer - ri - ly we roll a - long, O'er the deep blue sea.

BAA, BAA, BLACK SHEEP

Nursery Rhyme

J. W. Elliott

Baa, baa, black sheep, have you an - y wool? Yes sir, yes sir, three bags full.

One for my mas - ter and one for my dame, And one for the lit - tle boy that lives in the lane.

7. Play simple accompaniments to songs found in Appendix G (pages 169 to 213).

A series of tones arranged according to a definite plan within the octave form a musical scale (from the Latin word *scala,* meaning "ladder"). Most of our music is based on major and minor scales.[1] Both of these contain whole and half steps and are eight-tone, or diatonic, scales. Both are referred to as "modes" (from the Latin *modus,* meaning "form").

The Major-scale Pattern

If you sound only the white keys on the piano beginning and ending on C, you have played the major scale. Notice that half steps occur between the third and fourth tones (E and F) and between the seventh and eighth tones (B and C), where no black keys intervene. Elsewhere, black keys are between the white keys, thus making whole steps.

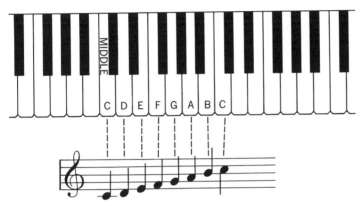

Scale numbers   1 2 3 4 5 6 7 8

A major scale may begin on any pitch, or key, of the piano, and it will sound the same as the C major scale provided you use certain black keys—that is, by means of sharps and flats, called "chromatics," you can make the necessary whole and half steps occur in the proper places.

Scale degrees (1)   (2)   (3)   (4)   (5)   (6)   (7)   (8)[2]
Step pattern   W   W   H   W   W   W   H

1. There are other scales, such as the chromatic, or half-tone, scale, which consists of all the white and black keys on the piano within the octave; the pentatonic, or five-tone, scale, which you can play on the black keys of the piano; and a whole-tone scale with six tones. Part of the chromatic scale often is used to embellish melodies. The pentatonic scale has been used by peoples of early and different cultures, such as the Chinese, Africans, Scots, and American Indians. You will hear it in some of the Negro spirituals and Scotch melodies you sing. The whole-tone scale was developed mainly by the French composer Claude Achille Debussy (1862–1918).

2. W = whole step; H = half step.

The Key of G Major

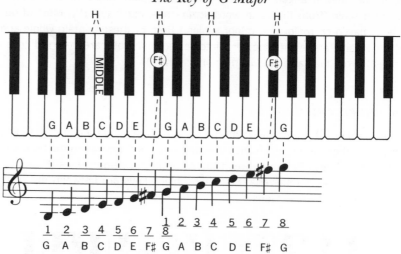

The Key of F Major

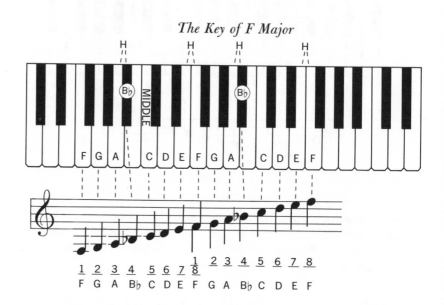

Tonal Characteristics

As you play and sing the scale, you should observe certain tonal characteristics. For example, the second, fourth, sixth, and seventh tones tend to move to, or are "pulled toward," the first, third, fifth, and eighth tones. They are known as the "active" tones, and the first, third, fifth, and eighth tones are the "rest" tones, the tones to which the active tones resolve. The resolution of active tones may not be immediate, however. Notice in the following sequence that it is delayed.

62

Major-key Signatures

When sharps and flats are needed to establish a scale, it is easier to group them at the beginning of each staff (just after the clef sign and before the meter signature) than to have them appear in every measure. This grouping, known as the "key signature," affects all notes on the degrees on which the sharps and flats appear for as long as the key signature remains the same.

In referring to a composition with a certain signature, we say that it is written in that particular key or has that tonality. In other words, the composition has a central tone around which the music gravitates. To illustrate, when we say a song or an instrumental composition is in the key of G, we mean that G is the basic, or focal, tone, the one from which the music departs and to which it returns, i.e., the scale built on G.

To find the key of a song written in major with the key signature in sharps, call the last sharp (the one farthest to the right) seven and count up one half step to eight. The staff degree on which this is located is the beginning note of the scale and the name of the key. In compositions written in major with flats in the signature, call the last flat four and count down to one. In major keys with more that one flat in the signature, the next to the last flat is the name of the key.[3]

Sharps and flats in the key signature are placed in order and in an exact manner:

Names for Scale Tones

In addition to the letter names of the staff degrees and numbers, the tones of the scale are designated by the Italian syllables *do, re, mi, fa, sol, la, ti, do* (pronounced *doh, ray, mee, fah, sol, lah, tee, doh*). These originated in the eleventh century when Guido d'Arezzo, a monk and choir director, discovered that each phrase of the hymn to St. John the Baptist began one pitch higher than the preceding one. He thereupon conceived the idea of using the initial syllable of each line to represent a six-tone scale.

63

---

3. Keys with six and seven sharps and flats are not given here since, as a rule, they are not used in elementary school songs.

Ut queant laxis
*Re*sonare fibris
*Mi*ra gestorum
*Fa*muli tuorum
*Sol*ve polluti
*La*bii reatum

The seventh tone (*ti*)[4] was introduced with the eight-tone scale in the six-teenth century. About 1670, the syllable *ut* was changed to *do*. The letter l is often omitted from *sol* in order to have all syllables end with an open vowel sound.

There are two plans of *sol-fa* syllables (*solmization*). One is the fixed *do*, where the syllables are alternate terms for the staff degree letters.[5] In this method, *do* always stands for C, *re* for D, *mi* for E, and so forth. In the movable *do* scheme (commonly used in American schools), *do* is always the first tone of the scale, *re* the second tone, *mi* the third tone, etc. It is, therefore, a tonality, or scale, plan.

do	re	mi	fa	sol	la	ti	do		do	re	mi	fa	sol	la	ti	do
1	2	3	4	5	6	7	8		1	2	3	4	5	6	7	8
C	D	E	F	G	A	B	C		D	E	F♯	G	A	B	C♯	D

In the *sol-fa* scale system, there are specific names for each scale tone. To form names for the ascending chromatic scale,[6] the vowel sounds are changed to i (sound of *ee* as in "see" or of *i* as in "machine"). In the descending form, the vowels become e (sound of *ay* as in "say" or of *ey* as in "they") except for the second degree of the scale, which becomes a (as in "ah"). The ascending scale names therefore are *do, di, re, ri, mi, fa, fi, sol, si, la, li, ti, do*. The descending scale names are *do, ti, te, la, le, sol, se, fa, mi, me, re, ra, do*.

Chromatic scale

| do | di | re | ri | mi | fa | fi | sol | si | la | li | ti | do |

| do | ti | te | la | le | sol | se | fa | mi | me | re | ra | do |

4. The seventh tone was first called *si* but was changed to *ti* with the introduction of the chromatic syllables.

5. The fixed *do* plan is used in some European schools. It is also in favor with some American instrumentalists and theoreticians.

It should be mentioned that there is controversy among music educators as to the value of the *sol-fa* syllables, regardless of the method. However, they are used in many elementary schools and, therefore, are included in this book.

6. See Footnote 1 on page 61.

When you sing songs where chromatics appear in a measure with scale numbers and degree letters, you *think* the chromatic term but do not *sing* it.

Example

My	coun - try,		'tis	of	thee
do	*do*	*re*	*ti*	*do*	*re*
1	1	2	7♯	1	2
G	G	A	F♯	G	A

Assignment

1. Write the step pattern for major scales.

2. **a** Play the major scale beginning on D, E♭, E, A, and B♭ on both the piano and the song bells.

    b Write these major scales in both treble and bass staffs, placing the sharps and flats before notes where needed. After you have done this, assemble these into the key signature.

3. Give rules for locating the first, or key, tone in sharp and flat keys.

4. As you sing familiar songs, such as "O Rest in the Lord" (page 9), "May Day Carol" (page 7), "The Little Sandman" (page 14), and "Evening Song" (page 24), notice where and how the active tones of the scale move.

5. What are the names for scale tones?

6. Discuss different methods of using *sol-fa* syllables (solmization). Which seems more practical to you, and why?

7. Memorize and write the *sol-fa* syllables both diatonic and chromatic.

8. Sing the following songs with syllables, numbers, and words. Name the key and the beginning and ending tones of each song.

    "Row, Row, Row Your Boat" (page 6)
    "Joy to the World" (page 6)
    "Old Folks at Home" (page 12)
    "Wait for the Wagon" (page 19)
    "The Quilting Party" (page 26)
    "Away in a Manger" (page 32)

9. Copy the song "Sweet and Low" (page 35), placing the *sol-fa* syllables, scale numbers, and degree names beneath the notes.

The Major and Minor Modes

Sing "Cockles and Mussels" (page 25). The first verse and the refrain of the song are in the major mode, but the second verse is in the minor mode. The minor scale, of which there are three forms (natural, harmonic, and melodic), differs from the major scale in its pattern of whole and half steps. Therefore, it is characteristically different in tonal effects. You will immediately recognize the minor mode when you play and sing the first three tones of the scale because the distance from the first to the third tone is one and one-half steps, whereas in the major it is two whole steps.

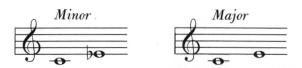

Parallel and Relative Minor Scales

Like the major scale, the minor scale can be constructed on any tone or any key of the piano provided the steps are arranged properly. When the minor scale begins on the same tone as a major scale, it is said to be "parallel" to it. The key signature is different, but the beginning and ending tones are the same. When the minor scale starts on the sixth tone of a major scale, it has the same key signature as the major and is called the "relative scale." The beginning and ending tones, however, are different.

G major

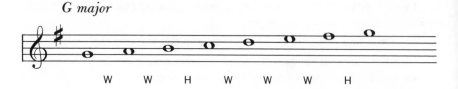

G minor (parallel minor of G major)

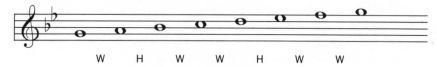

E minor (relative minor of G major)

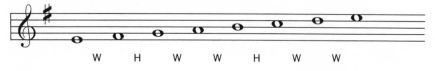

GO TELL AUNT RHODIE

Traditional American Song

G Major

Go tell Aunt Rho - die, Go tell Aunt Rho - die,

Go tell Aunt Rho - die The old gray goose is dead.

G Minor

Go tell Aunt Rho - die, Go tell Aunt Rho - die,

Go tell Aunt Rho - die The old gray goose is dead.

E Minor

Go tell Aunt Rho - die, Go tell Aunt Rho - die,

Go tell Aunt Rho - die The old gray goose is dead.

In order to avoid confusion, the discussion that follows will consider minor scales as relative to the major key.

Natural Minor Scale

When you begin and end on A both ascending and descending and playing only the white keys on the piano, you have played the natural minor scale. That is, this scale is formed by starting and ending on the sixth tone of the major scale without any chromatic changes.

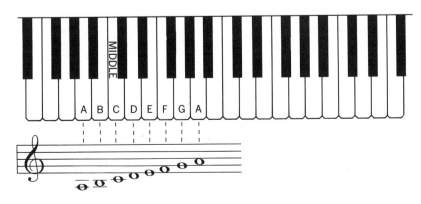

67

Major scale   *Natural minor scale*

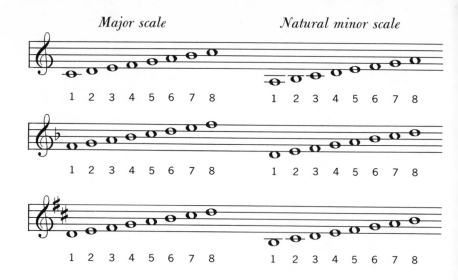

Natural minor

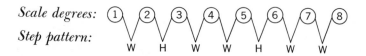

THE COAST OF HIGH BARBARY

Sea Chantey

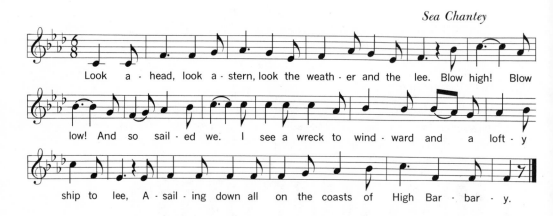

Look a - head, look a - stern, look the weath - er and the lee. Blow high! Blow low! And so sail - ed we. I see a wreck to wind - ward and a loft - y ship to lee, A - sail - ing down all on the coasts of High Bar - bar - y.

68

Harmonic Minor Scale

If you play the natural minor scale again beginning and ending on A but, instead of sounding G natural, play G sharp, you have formed the harmonic minor scale. In other words, to form the harmonic minor scale, the seventh tone is raised both ascending and descending and requires a chromatic before it. Notice the wide step between the sixth and seventh degrees (a step and a half).

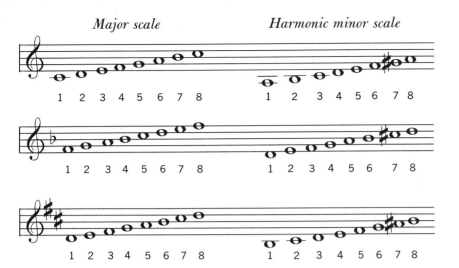

Major scale   *Harmonic minor scale*

Harmonic minor

Scale degrees: 1   2   3   4   5   6   7   8

Step pattern: W   H   W   W   H   W + H   H

JOSHUA FOUGHT THE BATTLE OF JERICHO

Negro Spiritual

Josh - ua fought the bat - tle of   Jer - i - cho,   Jer - i - cho,   Jer - i - cho;

Josh - ua fought the bat - tle of   Jer - i - cho, and the walls came tum - bl - ing down.

In the song "When Johnny Comes Marching Home" (page 33), the composer has used the natural minor scale in the first part of the song and the harmonic minor scale in the last part. Notice the G natural in the third and fourth measures and the G sharp in the next to the last measure.

69

Melodic Minor Scale

A third form of the minor scale is the "melodic." In the ascending order, the sixth and seventh tones are raised a half step; but in descending, they are lowered again, thus making the descending scale the same as the natural minor scale.

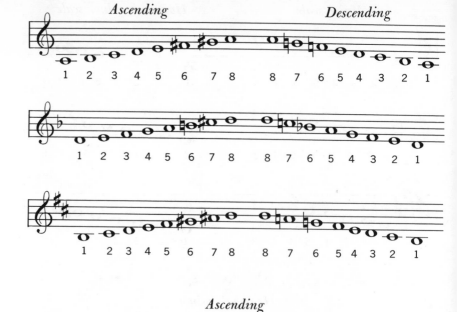

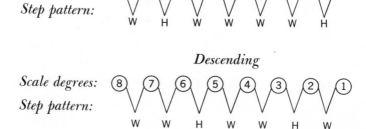

Additional chromatics (i.e., other than those in the key signature) needed to form the melodic minor scale are placed directly before the notes affected.

THE WATER SPRITE

Folk Song

1. On the rock, the crys - tal rock, re - clin - ing,
2. While the maid - ens of the night are twin - ing

Lies the Sprite in his sea - green hall.
Veils of gloom o - ver hill and dale.

THE CURFEW BELL

Folk Tune

Sol - emn - ly, mourn - ful - ly, deal - ing its dole, The
cur - few bell is be - gin - ning to toll.

Minor-key Signatures

You cannot tell from looking at the key signature whether the song is major or minor. A clue, however, is the ending note because most minor songs end on the sixth tone, or *la,* of the major scale. Sometimes the beginning tone also is the sixth degree, or *la,* of the major scale. Playing or singing a song, of course, will tell you if it is major or minor.[1]

Major

C   G   D   A   E   B

Minor

A   E   B   F#   C#   G#

Major

F   Bb   Eb   Ab   Db

Minor

D   G   C   F   Bb

1. The harmony used with the melody also reveals whether a song is major or minor.

Syllables and Numbers

The minor scales are diatonic scales (as are the major), and the beginning tone is 1. However, in singing with *sol-fa* syllables, it is easier to begin the scale with *la*, for that establishes the minor tonality naturally and easily (*la-ti-do*).

A—*Natural minor*

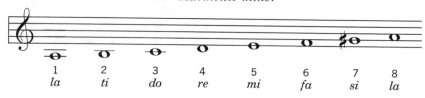

1	2	3	4	5	6	7	8
la	ti	do	re	mi	fa	sol	la

A—*Harmonic minor*

1	2	3	4	5	6	7	8
la	ti	do	re	mi	fa	si	la

A—*Melodic minor*

1	2	3	4	5	6	7	8	8	7	6	5	4	3	2	1
la	ti	do	re	mi	fi	si	la	la	sol	fa	mi	re	do	ti	la

Assignment

1. Sing within a comfortable range of your voice the different forms of the minor scale with numbers and with syllables. Play these scales on the piano and song bells, starting on three different pitches.

2. Name the different minor scales when you hear them played by your instructor or a member of the class.

3. Explain the terms "parallel minor scale" and "relative minor scale."

4. After singing the songs below, can you tell which form of the minor scale was used?

5. The minor mode has often been described as "sad." Do you think that this word applies to all these songs? What word or words would you use to describe the mood of each?

6. Name the key of each song and the beginning and ending tones.

7. Select two of the songs to conduct before the class.

8. Sing three of the songs with syllables.

9. Play four of the songs on the bells and piano.

GO DOWN, MOSES

Negro Spiritual

1. When Is - rael was in E - gypt's land, Let my peo - ple go, ___ Op -
2. Thus said the Lord, bold Mo - ses said, Let my peo - ple go. ___ If

press'd so hard they could not stand, Let my peo - ple go.
not, I'll smite your first - born dead! Let my peo - ple go.

Refrain

Go down, Mo - ses, 'Way down in E - gypt's land; Tell old Pha - raoh, ___ Let my peo - ple go!

OH, VERMELAND

Swedish Folk Song

1. Oh, Verm - e - land, the love - ly, thou glo - ri - ous land, From
2. Oh, Verm - e - land, the fair - est of all the lands of earth, And

thee ne - ver - more will I be roam - ing.
to thy land of green will I be com - ing.

THE JOLLY MILLER

English Folk Song

There was a jol - ly mill - er once liv'd on the Riv - er Dee, ___

He worked and sang from morn 'till night, No lark more blithe than he. ___

And this the bur - den of his song for - ev - er used to be: ___

"I care for no - bod - y, no, not I, If no - bod - y cares for me." ___

THE WRAGGLE-TAGGLE GYPSIES

Old English Ballad

1. There —— were three gyp - sies a - come to my door, And down - stairs ran
2. Then —— she pulled off her —— silk - fin - ish'd gown And put on hose

3. It was late last night when my lord came —— home, In - quir - ing for

this - a la - dy, O! The one sang high, and an - oth - er sang low,
of —— leath - er, O! The rag - ged rags a - bout —— our door,
his —— la - dy, O! The ser - vants said on —— ev - 'ry hand,

And the oth - er sang, "Bon - ny, bon - ny Bis - cay, O!"
And she's gone —— with the wrag - gle - tag - gle gyp - sies, O!
"She's gone —— with the wrag - gle - tag - gle gyp - sies, O!"

GREENSLEEVES

Moderately *English Folk Song*

1. A - las, my love, —— you do me wrong —— to cast me off —— dis - cour - teous - ly;
2. If you in - tend —— thus to dis - dain, —— it does the more —— en - rap - ture me,

And I have lov - ed you so long, —— de - light - ing in —— your com - pa - ny.
And e - ven so —— I still re - main —— a sweet - heart in —— cap - tiv - i - ty.

Chorus

Green - sleeves was all my joy, —— Green - sleeves —— was my de - light;

Green - sleeves was my heart of gold, —— and who but my la - dy Green-sleeves.

74

LULLABY

U. Bachmetieff

Sleep, ah sleep, my dar - ling ba - by, Su, su, lul - la - by; ____

See the moon is watch - ing o'er thee, Peace - ful - ly on high; ____

Thou shalt hear a won - drous sto - ry; Close each wake - ful eye, ____

And a song as well I'll sing thee, Su, su, lul - la - by. ____

CHARLIE IS MY DARLING

Scotch Folk Song

Refrain

Char - lie is my dar - ling, my dar - ling, my dar - ling, Oh

Fine

Char - lie is my dar - ling, The young Chev - a - lier.

1. Twas on a Mon - day morn - ing, Right ear - ly in the year, When
2. As he came march - ing up the street, The pipes played loud and clear, And

Char - lie came to our town, The young Chev - a - lier, Oh! ____
all the folks came run - ning out To meet the Chev - a - lier, Oh! ____

75

A WAYFARING STRANGER

Spiritual

I'm just a poor way-far-ing stran-ger While trav-'ling through this world of
woe; I'm go-ing there to see my fa-ther, I'm go-ing home no more to
roam; I'm on-ly go-ing o-ver Jor-dan, I'm on-ly go-ing o-ver home.

THE ORGAN-GRINDER*

Wilhelm Müller   *Franz Schubert*

Up be-hind the vil-lage stands an or-gan man,
No one lis-tens to him, no one looks or cares,

And with stiff-en'd fin-gers turns as best he can;
Snar-ling dogs pur-sue him, still a smile he wears;

On the cold ground, bare-foot, si-dles here and there,
And no dis-ap-point-ment does he once be-tray,

And his emp-ty sau-cer shows the gifts are rare,
But up-on the or-gan turns and turns a-way,

And his emp-ty sau-cer shows the gifts are rare.
But up-on the or-gan turns and turns a-way.

D.C.

Won-der-ful old min-strel, shall I go with you?

Fine

Will you to my dit-ties play the mu-sic, too?_____

76

An "interval" is the difference in pitch between two tones. The smallest interval in our music is a half step (half tone). A knowledge and awareness of pitch relationship are important to your understanding of scale structure, melody, and harmony.

Melodic and Harmonic Intervals

When pitches are sounded successively, the difference between them is a "melodic interval." When sounded simultaneously, the difference is a "harmonic interval."[1]

Measurement and Names of Intervals

Intervals are named numerically according to the number of staff degrees or letter names involved, reckoning from the lower to the higher. For example, to find the interval from C to F, count the beginning and ending notes, or staff degrees, which is four. Therefore, C to F is an interval of a fourth. The interval between E and B is a fifth because five degrees or letters are involved.

The numerical name of an interval always remains the same even though its size may vary by means of sharps and flats. The interval from C to E is a third, as is the interval from C to E♭. But they are not the same size, and they do not sound the same. C to E is two whole steps, whereas C to E♭ is only a step and a

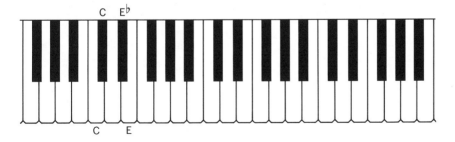

half. Hence, in addition to the numerical classification, specific names are used to describe the interval more accurately. The standard of measurement is the major scale. The lower note of the interval is always considered as the beginning note of a major scale. If the second note occurs within the scale, the interval is

1. You will find the intervals of a third and sixth sound well together and are used frequently in two-part singing.

a perfect fourth, fifth, unison, or octave; or it is a major second, third, sixth, or seventh. When lowered by a half step, perfect intervals become diminished intervals and major intervals become minor. When made larger by a half step, minor intervals become major and major and perfect intervals become augmented intervals.[2] Although all intervals can be augmented and diminished doubly and more, the information given here will be sufficient for your purposes.

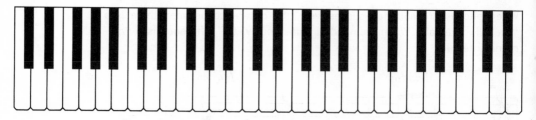

All intervals can be built starting on any tone of the scale and in any key.[3] The key of C is used in the following illustration.

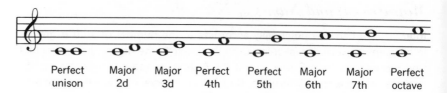

| Perfect unison | Major 2d | Major 3d | Perfect 4th | Perfect 5th | Major 6th | Major 7th | Perfect octave |

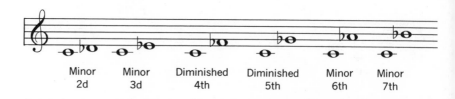

| Minor 2d | Minor 3d | Diminished 4th | Diminished 5th | Minor 6th | Minor 7th |

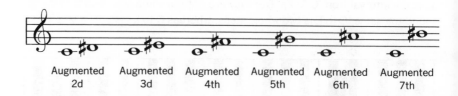

| Augmented 2d | Augmented 3d | Augmented 4th | Augmented 5th | Augmented 6th | Augmented 7th |

Assignment

1. What are intervals in music, and how are they measured and named?

2. Play the intervals on this page. Sing them with degree names and syllables.

3. You can identify and easily sing various intervals by relating them to familiar songs. For example, "Oh, Susanna" (page 15) begins with major seconds. Throughout the song "Wait for the Wagon" (page 19), you will find perfect

---

2. Intervals larger than the octave are reduced to their equivalent within the octave, ninths becoming seconds, tenths becoming thirds, etc.

3. An augmented unison (prime) plays the same notes on the piano as the minor second, the augmented second as the minor third, the augmented third as the perfect fourth, etc.

octaves. "The Star-Spangled Banner" (page 22) begins with a descending minor third followed by a major third. The song "Greensleeves" (page 74) begins with an ascending minor third. The aria "O Rest in the Lord" (page 9) begins with a major third. Play, then sing the beginning intervals of these songs with numbers and syllables.

With what intervals do the following songs begin? Play, then sing them with words, numbers, and syllables.

"All through the Night" (page 5)
"Vesper Hymn" (page 7)
"The Little Sandman" (page 14)
"Flow Gently, Sweet Afton" (page 16)
"Weel May the Keel Row" (page 33)
"When Johnny Comes Marching Home" (page 33)
"Go Down, Moses" (page 73)
"Joshua Fought the Battle of Jericho" (page 69)

4.   What interval is repeated in the refrain of "My Bonnie"? Give the specific name. How many intervals of a sixth are found in "Jingle Bells"? Are they major or minor? Find the intervals of ascending seconds and sevenths in "Sing a Song of Sixpence" and the sevenths in "From Lucerne to Weggis." Are they major or minor? Give the rule for determining this. Sing these intervals with numbers and syllables.

MY BONNIE

Old Song

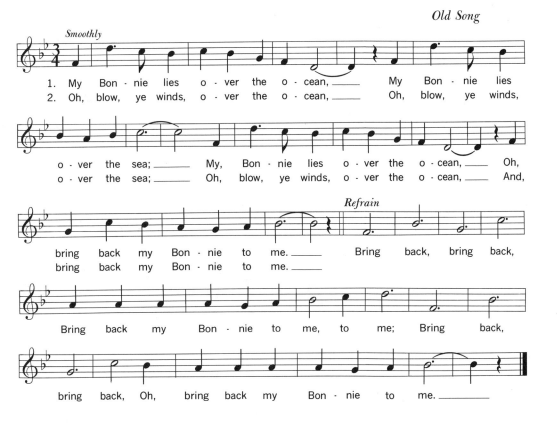

79

JINGLE BELLS

J. Pierpont

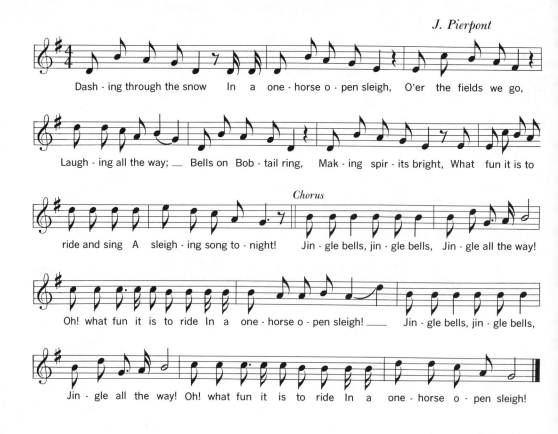

Dash - ing through the snow   In a one - horse o - pen sleigh, O'er the fields we go,

Laugh - ing all the way; __ Bells on Bob - tail ring,   Mak - ing spir - its bright, What fun it is to

Chorus

ride and sing A sleigh - ing song to - night!   Jin - gle bells, jin - gle bells, Jin - gle all the way!

Oh! what fun it is to ride In a one - horse o - pen sleigh! __   Jin - gle bells, jin - gle bells,

Jin - gle all the way! Oh! what fun it is to ride In a   one - horse o - pen sleigh!

SING A SONG OF SIXPENCE

Mother Goose

J. W. Elliott

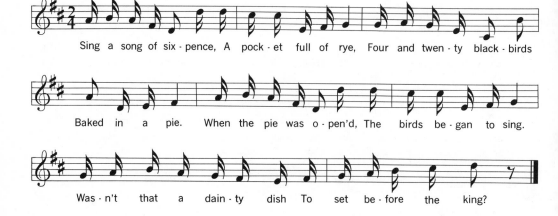

Sing a song of six - pence, A pock - et full of rye, Four and twen - ty black - birds

Baked in a pie.   When the pie was o - pen'd, The   birds be - gan to sing.

Was - n't that a dain - ty dish To set be - fore the king?

FROM LUCERNE TO WEGGIS

Martha Dabney

Swiss Folk Tune

1. Up the hill and ___ down the way, Hol-di-ri-di-a hol-di-ri-a,
2. No more shoes than ___ fish-es wear, Hol-di-ri-di-a hol-di-ri-a,
3. Bare-foot as the ___ birds we'll roam, Hol-di-ri-di-a hol-di-ri-a,

We shall wear no ___ shoes to-day, Hol-di-ri-di-a hol-di-a.
In the brook that ___ wan-ders near, Hol-di-ri-di-a hol-di-a.
Up the hills and ___ down, and home, Hol-di-ri-di-a hol-di-a.

From *New Music Horizons*, Book Five. Copyright 1946, 1953, Silver Burdett Company, Morristown, N. J. Used by permission.

5. Play the following sequence of intervals in the keys of C, A, and Bb. Sing them in these keys with numbers and syllables. Give the specific interval names, as "C to E is a major third, D to F is a minor third," and so forth.

Harmony

Harmony, an important element of music, is the simultaneous sounding of three or more tones. It gives substance and richness to melody if the right combinations are used. When groups of tones, called "triads" or " chords," blend and give an effect of repose, they are said to be consonant. If, on the other hand, one or more tones that seemingly do not belong are slipped into a chord, they give a feeling of tension or unrest and bring about dissonance. The chord is then an "active chord," which needs eventually to move to a consonant one for completion. Dissonant chords are not necessarily unpleasant. Indeed, they add color and interest to music.

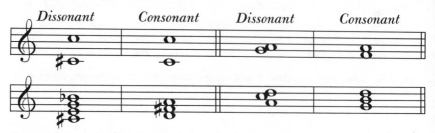

Polyphonic and Homophonic Music

Although harmony consists of chords of three or more tones, two tones played or sung together can make harmonious sounds, as in two-part singing. One tune sung with another when the tones agree or are consonant for the most part (called "descant") and some melodies which begin with one voice and are repeated by one or more voices at a given distance (as in rounds and canons) also make pleasing tonal combinations.

When singing rounds and canons, notice how the voices enter one after the other, each singing the melody at a designated time. Notice, too, how all these weave together to make an interesting musical pattern of sounds. This music is called "contrapuntal" (literally, "note against note") or "polyphonic" (many voices). On the other hand, music in which one voice or melody stands out or is supported by chords or other subordinate material is known as "homophonic."[1]

Singing in Parts

Some of you may have an instinctive feeling for harmony and can improvise parts to familiar melodies. Some of you, however, may have to acquire a sensitivity to it by training your ears to hear tones separately and together; you may also have to learn to control your voice so that you can produce any part in tonal groupings. Rounds, canons, and descants are a useful introduction to part singing, and it may be helpful if the class sings isolated combinations of tones and the chords in the final cadences of songs. To intone or sing repeated tones (to chant) against a melody also is an easy beginning to part singing.[2]

1. A composition for a single voice without parts or chordal accompaniment is called "monophonic" (one sound) music. It is the oldest form of music and is exemplified in early Greek music and in Gregorian chants. Polyphonic, homophonic, and monophonic music are often referred to as the "texture" of music.

2. Instrumental accompaniments, especially those of a chordal nature, provide an excellent harmonic background.

part singing

11

suggestions

1. The instructor should divide the class into sections for part singing.

2. All parts must blend or harmonize to make a musically unified whole. Therefore, you should listen carefully to other parts and not just to the one which you are singing.

3. Sing alternate parts on alternate songs so that you learn to "carry" a part easily and well.

4. Parts may be played on instruments before you sing them.

5. Part songs should be sung by small groups as well as by the entire class.

6. Practice singing parts with vowels, syllables (*lah, no*, etc.), *sol-fa* syllables, and words.

Assignment

1. Explain the following: harmony, consonant, dissonant, polyphonic, homophonic.

2. Try to extemporize a lower part as the rest of the class sings the melody to "Joy to the World," "Old Folks at Home" (refrain), "The Quilting Party," or other familiar songs.

3. Listen to the following tonal combinations as they are played on the piano or song bells; then sing the part assigned you. (Sing with the sound *ah* and *sol-fa* syllables.)

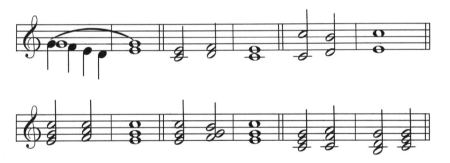

4. Play the following song endings on the piano or song bells; then select a small group of your classmates to sing them with you. Play and sing them in three different keys and learn to sing each part.

83

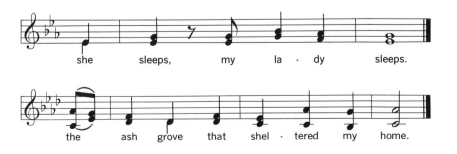

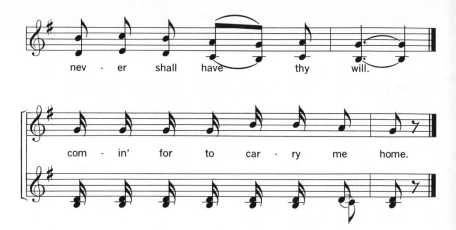

nev - er shall have thy will.

com - in' for to car - ry me home.

5. *Rounds and canons.* Rounds should first be sung several times as unison songs. Then the class should be divided into two or more groups. When the first group gets to the measure marked **2**, the second group should start at the measure marked **1**; and when the second group gets to the measure marked **2**, a third group may start on **1**, etc. A round should be sung at least twice when there are two divisions and three times when there are three groups of singers. Rounds marked for three or more groups may, however, be sung only by two groups.

The canon also should be played or sung as a unison song until the melody is familiar.

ARE YOU SLEEPING, BROTHER JOHN?

French Round

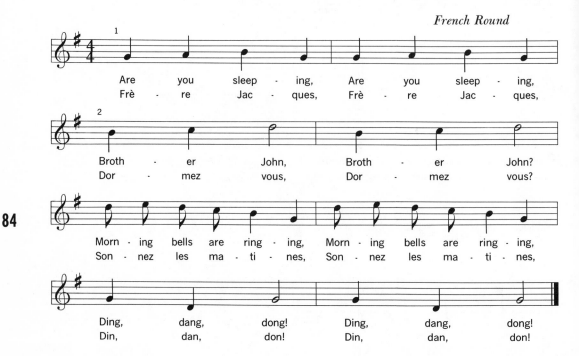

Are you sleep - ing, Are you sleep - ing,
Frè - re Jac - ques, Frè - re Jac - ques,

Broth - er John, Broth - er John?
Dor - mez vous, Dor - mez vous?

Morn - ing bells are ring - ing, Morn - ing bells are ring - ing,
Son - nez les ma - ti - nes, Son - nez les ma - ti - nes,

Ding, dang, dong! Ding, dang, dong!
Din, dan, don! Din, dan, don!

84

LOVELY EVENING

Traditional Round

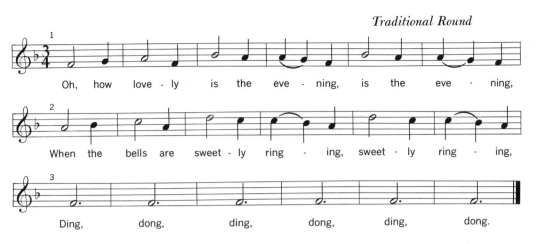

Oh, how love - ly is the eve - ning, is the eve - ning,

When the bells are sweet - ly ring - ing, sweet - ly ring - ing,

Ding, dong, ding, dong, ding, dong.

ROW, ROW, ROW YOUR BOAT

E. O. Lyte

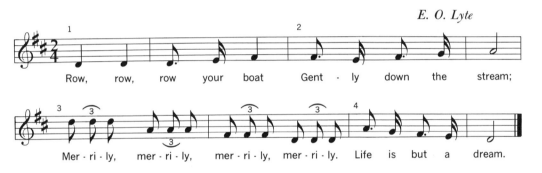

Row, row, row your boat Gent - ly down the stream;

Mer - ri - ly, mer - ri - ly, mer - ri - ly, mer - ri - ly. Life is but a dream.

SING TOGETHER

Round

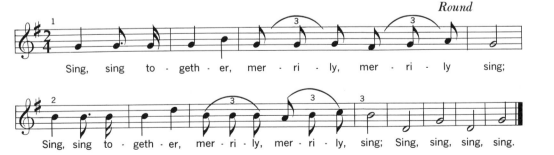

Sing, sing to - geth - er, mer - ri - ly, mer - ri - ly sing;

Sing, sing to - geth - er, mer - ri - ly, mer - ri - ly, sing; Sing, sing, sing, sing.

85

DONA NOBIS PACEM[3]

Three-part Round

Andante

Do - na no - bis pa - cem, pa - cem;

do - na _____ no - bis pa - cem.

Do - na no - bis pa - cem;

do - na no - bis pa - cem.

Do - na no - bis _____ pa - cem;

do - na no - bis pa - cem.

PRAYER CANON

Thomas Ken

Thomas Tallis

We thank Thee, Fa - ther, for the night, For all the bless - ings

We thank Thee, Fa - ther, for the night, For

of the light; Keep us, O keep us. King of Kings, Be -

all the bless - ings of the light; Keep us, O keep us,

3. Translation: "Give us peace."

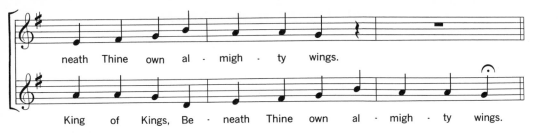

neath Thine own al - migh - ty wings.

King of Kings, Be - neath Thine own al - migh - ty wings.

6. *Descants.* Only a few soprano voices should sing the descant.

THE FIRST NOWELL

Traditional

1. The _____ first _____ Now - ell, the _____ an - gel did say,
2. They _____ look - ed _____ up and _____ saw _____ a star

Was to cer - tain poor shep - herds in fields as they lay,
Shin - ing in _____ the East _____ be - yond them a - far,

In _____ fields _____ where _____ they lay _____ keep - ing their sheep
And _____ to _____ the _____ earth it _____ gave a great light,

On a cold win - ter's night _____ that was _____ so deep.
And _____ so it con - tin - ued both day _____ and night.

Descant

Now - ell, _____ Now - ell, Now - ell, _____ Now - ell, _____

87

Born is the King _____ of Is - ra - el.

From *New Music Horizons*, Book Five. Copyright 1946, 1953, Silver Burdett Company, Morristown, N.J. Used by permission.

ALL THROUGH THE NIGHT

Quietly

Welsh Folk Song

Descant

Loo, _____ Loo, _____

Loo, _____ Loo, _____

1. Sleep, my child, and peace at-tend thee All through the night,
2. While the moon her watch is keep-ing All through the night,

Guar - dian an - gels God will send thee All through the night,
While the wea - ry world is sleep - ing All through the night,

Loo, _____ Loo, _____

Soft the drow - sy hours are creep - ing, Hill and vale in slum - ber steep - ing,
O'er thy spir - it gent - ly steal - ing, Vis - ions of de - light re - veal - ing,

Loo, _____ All through the night.

I my lov - ing vig - il keep - ing All through the night.
Breathes a pure and ho - ly feel - ing All through the night.

7. Chants

SARASPONDA

88

Spinning Song

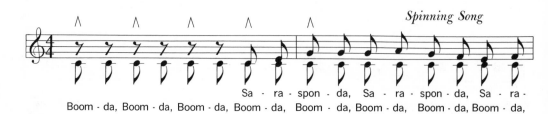

Sa - ra - spon - da, Sa - ra - spon - da, Sa - ra -
Boom - da, Boom - da, Boom - da, Boom - da, Boom - da, Boom - da, Boom - da, Boom - da,

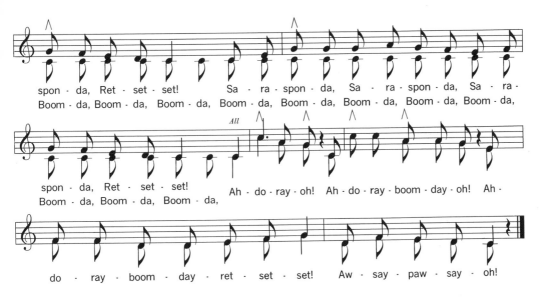

spon - da, Ret - set - set! Sa - ra - spon - da, Sa - ra - spon - da, Sa - ra -
Boom - da, Boom - da, Boom - da, Boom - da, Boom - da, Boom - da, Boom - da, Boom - da,

spon - da, Ret - set - set! Ah - do - ray - oh! Ah - do - ray - boom - day - oh! Ah -
Boom - da, Boom - da, Boom - da,

do - ray - boom - day - ret - set - set! Aw - say - paw - say - oh!

Sing the "Boom-da" softly to represent the sound of the spinning wheel.

ZUM GALI GALI

Palestinian Song

1. He - cha - lutz   le   'man   a - vo - dah; _____
2. A - vo - dah   le   'man   he - cha - lutz; _____
3. He - cha - lutz   le   'man   ha - b'tu - la; _____
4. Ha - sha - lom   le   'man   ha' - a - mim; _____

Zum   ga - li   ga - li   ga - li,   Zum   ga - li   ga - li,

_____ A - vo - dah   le   'man   he - cha - lutz.
_____ He - cha - lutz   le   'man   a - vo - dah.
_____ Ha - b'tu - lah   le   'man   he - cha - lutz.
_____ Ha' - a - mim   le   'man   ha - sha - lom.

Zum   ga - li   ga - li   ga - li,   Zum   ga - li   ga - li.

89

From *Joyful Singing*, n.d., Cooperative Recreation Service, Delaware, Ohio. Used by permission.

An approximate translation of the Hebrew words is:
   1 and 2. The pioneer's purpose is for labor.
   3. The pioneer is for his girl; his girl is for the pioneer.
   4. Peace for all the nations.
Pronunciation: *a* as in "father"; *he* as in "hay"; *le* with short *e* as in "end"; *i* as in "machine"; *o* as in "come"; *u* as in "rule"; *ch* as in the German *ach*.

8. *Two-part songs*

TELL ME WHY

College Song

Melody

Tell me why the stars do shine, Tell me why the iv - y twines,

Tell me why the skies are blue, And I will tell you why I love you.

STARS OF THE SUMMER NIGHT

Henry W. Longfellow *Isaac B. Woodbury*

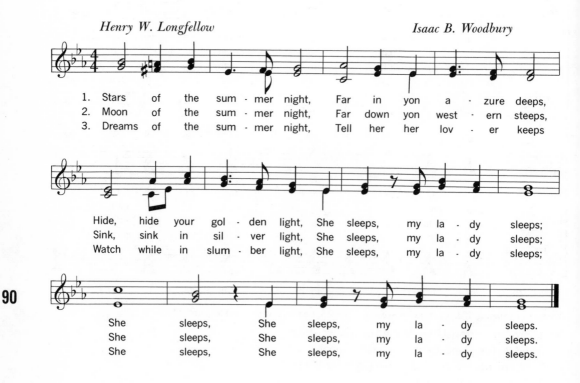

1. Stars of the sum - mer night, Far in yon a - zure deeps,
2. Moon of the sum - mer night, Far down yon west - ern steeps,
3. Dreams of the sum - mer night, Tell her her lov - er keeps

Hide, hide your gol - den light, She sleeps, my la - dy sleeps;
Sink, sink in sil - ver light, She sleeps, my la - dy sleeps;
Watch while in slum - ber light, She sleeps, my la - dy sleeps;

She sleeps, She sleeps, my la - dy sleeps.
She sleeps, She sleeps, my la - dy sleeps.
She sleeps, She sleeps, my la - dy sleeps.

THE ASH GROVE

John Oxenford   Welsh Folk Song

The ash grove, how grace - ful, how plain - ly 'tis speak - ing, The
When o - ver its branch - es the sun - light is break - ing, The

wind through it play - ing has lan - guage for me: The friends of my
host of kind fac - es is gaz - ing on me.

child - hood a - gain are be - fore me, Fond mem - o - ries wak - en as

free - ly I roam. With soft whis - pers la - den, the leaves rus - tle

o'er me; The ash grove, the ash grove that shel - tered my home.

BEGONE, DULL CARE

English Folk Song of the 17th Century

Be - gone, dull care; _____ I prith - ee, be - gone from me! _____ Be -

gone, dull care! You and I _____ shall nev - er a - gree. Long

time hast thou been tar - rying here, And fain thou would'st me kill, _____

But in faith, dull care, _____ Thou nev - er shall have thy will. _____

91

RED RIVER VALLEY

Old American Song

Hum

Solo voice

1. From this val · ley they say you are go · ing; We will
2. Won't you think of the val · ley you're leav · ing? Oh, how
3. Come and sit by my side if you love me; Do not

miss your bright eyes and sweet smile, For they say you are tak · ing the
lone · ly, how sad it will be. Oh, think of the fond heart you're
has · ten to bid me a · dieu. But re · mem · ber the Red Riv · er

sun · shine That bright · en'd our path · way a · while.
break · ing And the grief you are caus · ing me to see.
Val · ley And the girl that has loved you so true.

MORNING SONG

Franz Liszt

Moderato

1. The stars are slow · ly dy · ing, With all their gol · den light, But
2. Now reign · eth per · fect still · ness O'er val · ley, hill, and dale, And

as the night is fly - ing, The morn - ing dawn - eth bright.
thro' the cool sweet si - lence, Low sings the night - in - gale.

THE THREE RAVENS

English Song of the 16th Century

1. There were three ra - vens on a tree, Down a down, hey down, hey down! They
2. Be - hold, a - las, in yon green field, Down a down, hey down, hey down! There

were as black as they might be, With a down, a down, hey
lies a knight slain 'neath his shield, With a down, a down, hey

down, hey down. And one of them said to his mate, "Oh! where shall we our
down, hey down. His hounds lie down be - side his feet, So well do they their

break - fast take?" With a down der - ry der - ry, der - ry down, down.
mas - ter keep, With a down der - ry der - ry, der - ry down, down.

93

SWING LOW, SWEET CHARIOT

Negro Spiritual

Swing low, sweet char-i-ot, Com-in' for to car-ry me home;

Swing low, sweet char-i-ot, Com-in' for to car-ry me home.

1. I look'd o-ver Jor-dan an' what did I see, Com-in' for to car-ry me home?
2. If you get there be-fore I do, Com-in' for to car-ry me home,

A band of an-gels com-in' aft-er me, Com-in' for to car-ry me home.
Tell all my friends I'm com-in', too, Com-in' for to car-ry me home.

LAST NIGHT THE NIGHTINGALE WOKE ME

H. Kjerulf

94

Last night the night-in-gale woke me, Last night when

all was still; _____ It sang in the gol - den moon - light, From

out _____ the wood - land hill. I o - pen'd my win - dow so

gent - ly, I look'd on the dream - ing dew, _____ And oh, the

bird, my dar - ling, Was sing - ing sing - ing of you, of you.

WHICH IS THE PROPEREST DAY TO SING?

Dr. Thomas Augustine Arne
Arr. by W. G. McNaught

Spiritoso

Which is the pro - per - est day to sing? Sat - ur - day, Sun - day, Mon - day?

Which is the pro - per - est day to sing? Sat - ur - day, Sun - day, Mon - day?

Each to be sure, 'tis a might-y fine thing! Why should I name but one day?

Each to be sure, 'tis a might-y fine thing! Why should I name but one day?

Tell me but yours, I'll men-tion my day, Let us but fix on some day,

Tell me but yours, I'll men-tion my day, Let us but fix on some day,

Why, why? why should I name but one day?

Tell me but yours, I'll men-tion my day, Why should I name but one day?

Tell me but yours, I'll men-tion my day, Why should I name but one day?

Why, why, why, why? Why should I name but one day?

Each to be sure, 'tis a might-y fine thing! Let us but fix on some day.

Each to be sure, 'tis a might-y fine thing! Let us but fix on some day.

Which, which, which, which? Why should I name but one day?

96

Tues - day, Wednes - day, Bra - vo! Why should I name but one day?

Tues - day, Wednes - day, Thurs - day, Fri - day, Sat - ur - day, Sun - day, Mon - day,

Bra - vo! Thurs - day, Fri - day, Why should I name but one day?

Tues - day, Wednes - day, Thurs - day, Fri - day, Sat - ur - day, Sun - day, Mon - day,

Tues - day, Wednes - day, Thurs - day, Fri - day, Sat - ur - day, Sun - day, Mon - day,

Tues - day, Wednes - day, Thurs - day, Fri - day, Sat - ur - day, Sun - day, Mon - day,

Tues - day, Thurs - day, Sat - ur - day, Mon - day,

Which is the pro - per - est day to sing? Sat - ur - day, Sun - day, Mon - day,

Wednes - day, Fri - day, Sun - day, Mon - day,

Tues - day, Wednes - day, Thurs - day, Fri - day, Sat - ur - day, Sun - day, Mon - day.

Tues - day, Wednes - day, Thurs - day, Fri - day, Sat - ur - day, Sun - day, Mon - day.

97

Tues - day, Wednes - day, Thurs - day, Fri - day, Sat - ur - day, Sun - day, Mon - day.

Additional part songs can be found in books for the fifth and sixth grades in the basic Elementary Song Series. For list of the series, see Appendix F (page 168).

Chords and Their Names

The simplest chords in harmony are made up of three tones at intervals of a third, one on top of the other. These triads may be constructed on any tone of the scale, and each gets its name and number from the scale tone on which it is built.[1]

I	Tonic (1 or *do*)		V	Dominant (5 or *sol*)
ii	Supertonic (2 or *re*)		vi	Submediant (6 or *la*)
iii	Mediant (3 or *mi*)		vii	Leading tone (7 or *ti*)
IV	Subdominant (4 or *fa*)			

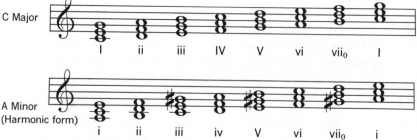

The top tone of the triad is a perfect fifth (*do-sol*) from the root, or beginning, tone in both major and minor triads with the exception of the one built on the leading tone. In this triad, the top tone is a diminished fifth from the fundamental tone and a minor third from the middle tone. It therefore consists of two superimposed minor thirds and is called a "diminished triad" (vii_0).

Major and Minor Chords

The middle tone determines whether the triad is major or minor. It is major if there are two whole steps between it and the root, or fundamental, tone of the chord, as when you sing *do-mi, fa-la, sol-ti*. It is minor if there are only one and one-half steps, as when you sing *re-fa, mi-sol, la-do, ti-re*.

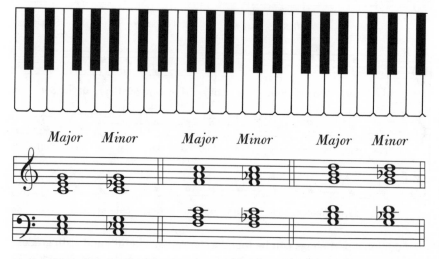

1. To indicate clearly the major and minor chords, large Roman numerals are used for major chords and small Roman numerals for minor chords.

Basic Chords

Although there are seven chords and variations of them, only three are needed to harmonize most school songs—the chord built on the first tone of the scale (tonic, or I), the chord built on the fourth tone (subdominant, or IV), and the chord built on the fifth tone (dominant, or V).

Dominant Seventh Chords

The dominant, or V, chord is frequently strengthened and enriched by adding a fourth tone which is a minor seventh from the fundamental tone. This is called a "dominant seventh chord" and is designated V_7. For ease in playing, the third tone of the chord usually is omitted.

Arrangements of Chords

The notes of chords can be arranged in different ways without altering the basic character. That is, a chord is tonic (I), subdominant (IV), or dominant (V) no matter how the tones are placed or doubled. A triad, for example, may have the third as the lowest tone of a grouping (the first inversion), with the root, or fundamental, tone as the highest; or it may have the fifth tone as the lowest (the second inversion), with the third tone as the highest. These inversions keep the hand movement to a minimum on the piano.

99

Tones need not necessarily be sounded simultaneously to give the effect of a chord.[2]

SILENT NIGHT

Franz Gruber

Si - lent night, Ho - ly night, All is calm, All is bright,

Round yon Vir - gin Moth - er and Child, Ho - ly In - fant so ten - der and mild,

Sleep in heav - en - ly peace, _____ Sleep in heav - en - ly peace. _____

100

2. These are called "arpeggios" (broken chords). For other chordal arrangements, see Appendix E (page 167).

TWINKLE, TWINKLE, LITTLE STAR

Traditional

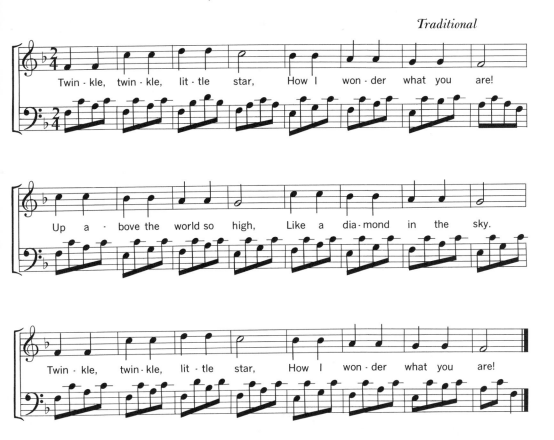

Twin - kle, twin - kle, lit - tle star, How I won - der what you are!

Up a - bove the world so high, Like a dia - mond in the sky.

Twin - kle, twin - kle, lit - tle star, How I won - der what you are!

When singers know and sing the melody independently, a satisfactory and easy accompaniment can be provided by playing the chords with the right hand and the fundamental tones of the chords with the left hand.

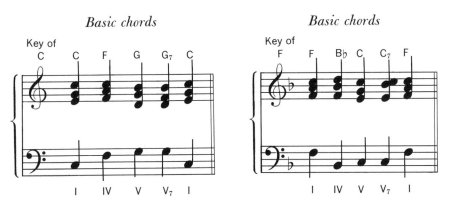

Basic chords

Key of C

C F G G₇ C

I IV V V₇ I

Basic chords

Key of F

F B♭ C C₇ F

I IV V V₇ I

101

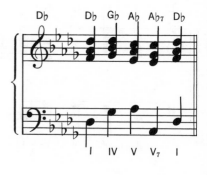

102

From *New Music Horizons,* Book Five. Copyright 1946, 1953, Silver Burdett Company, Morristown, N.J. Used by permission.

SILENT NIGHT

Franz Gruber

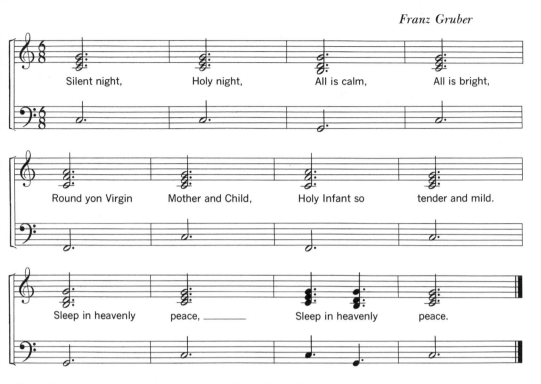

Silent night,   Holy night,   All is calm,   All is bright,

Round yon Virgin   Mother and Child,   Holy Infant so   tender and mild.

Sleep in heavenly   peace, _____   Sleep in heavenly   peace.

When the right hand plays the melody, the left hand plays the chords.

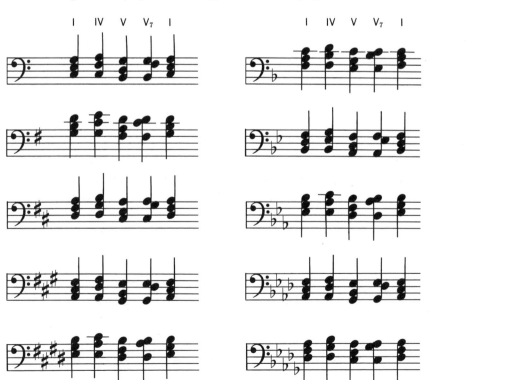

103

TWINKLE, TWINKLE, LITTLE STAR

Traditional

Twin-kle, twin-kle, lit-tle star, How I won-der what you are!

Up a-bove the world so high, Like a dia-mond in the sky.

Twin-kle, twin-kle, lit-tle star, How I won-der what you are!

SILENT NIGHT

Franz Gruber

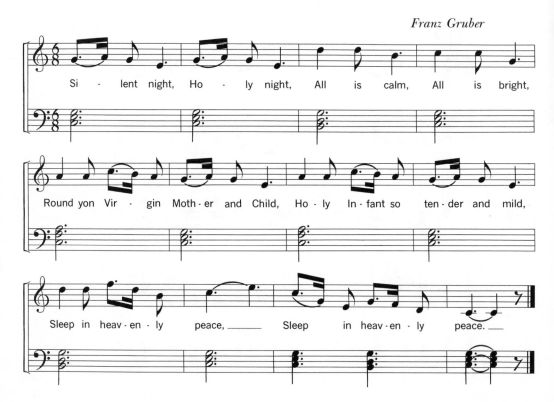

Si - lent night, Ho - ly night, All is calm, All is bright,

Round yon Vir - gin Moth-er and Child, Ho-ly In-fant so ten-der and mild,

Sleep in heav-en-ly peace, _____ Sleep in heav-en-ly peace. _____

104

ROW, ROW, ROW YOUR BOAT

E. O. Lyte

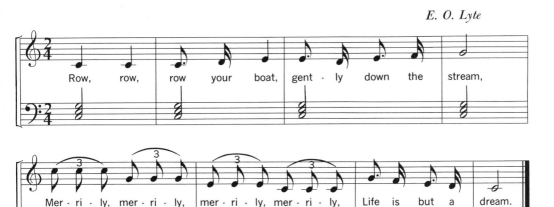

Row, row, row your boat, gent - ly down the stream,

Mer - ri - ly, mer - ri - ly, mer - ri - ly, mer - ri - ly, Life is but a dream.

How to Select Chords

To select the correct chords to use with a melody, first find the key. Next, number the scale tones in each measure. When a majority of the tones are part of the tonic, or I, chord (1-3-5), use that chord for the harmony. When a measure has a majority of tones belonging to the subdominant, or IV, chord (4-6-8), use that chord; and when the tones are chiefly those of the dominant or dominant seventh, V or V₇, chord (5-7-2 or 5-7-2-4), use either the V or V₇ chord.

Sometimes you will need to use more than one chord in a measure. Often, however, you need not harmonize every tone to make the harmonization sound well. As a rule, if a measure can be harmonized with the chord used in the preceding measure, you should retain that tonal grouping. The progression of chords should be I to IV to V or V₇ to I; I to IV to I; I to V or V₇ to I. The subdominant (IV) chord should not immediately follow the dominant or dominant seventh (V or V₇) chord. You should experiment with chord structure and chord progressions. Your ears generally will tell you when you have made the right selection.

example

THE FARMER IN THE DELL

Singing Game

The farm - er in the dell, _____ The farm - er in the dell, _____

Heigh, ho! the der - ry, oh, The farm - er in the dell. _____

Assignment

1. How are chords constructed and named?

2. Play the triads constructed on each scale tone in the key of C.

3. Write triads beginning on each scale tone in the keys of F and G major and in the key of A minor in both treble and bass staff; then play them.

4. Which are the "fundamental" chords? Learn to recognize these when you hear your instructor or a member of the class play them.

5. Practice the chords and songs on pages 101 to 104.

6. How do you determine which chord to play with a melody?

7. Follow these directions and play the following melodies with chordal accompaniment:

"Vesper Hymn" (page 7)
"Oh, Susanna" (page 15)
"Wait for the Wagon" (page 19)
"The Dairy Maids" (page 19)

LIGHTLY ROW

German Folk Tune

Light - ly row! Light - ly row! O'er the glass - y waves we go; Smooth - ly glide!

Smooth - ly glide! On the si - lent tide. Let the winds and wa - ters be

Min - gled with our mel - o - dy. Sing and float! Sing and float! In our lit - tle boat.

THE MUFFIN MAN

Singing Game

Joyfully

1. O do you know the muf - fin man, The muf - fin man, the muf - fin man; O
2. O yes, I know the muf - fin man, The muf - fin man, the muf - fin man; O

do you know the muf - fin man That lives in Dru - ry Lane?
yes, I know the muf - fin man That lives in Dru - ry Lane.

106

OLD SMOKY

Old American Song

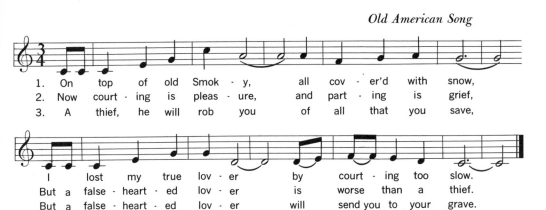

1. On top of old Smok - y, all cov - er'd with snow,
   I lost my true lov - er by court - ing too slow.
2. Now court - ing is pleas - ure, and part - ing is grief,
   But a false - heart - ed lov - er is worse than a thief.
3. A thief, he will rob you of all that you save,
   But a false - heart - ed lov - er will send you to your grave.

4. The grave will decay you
   and turn you to dust;
   Not a boy in ten thousand
   a poor girl can trust.

5. On top of old Smoky,
   all cover'd with snow,
   I lost my true lover
   by courting too slow.

OLD MACDONALD HAD A FARM

Traditional

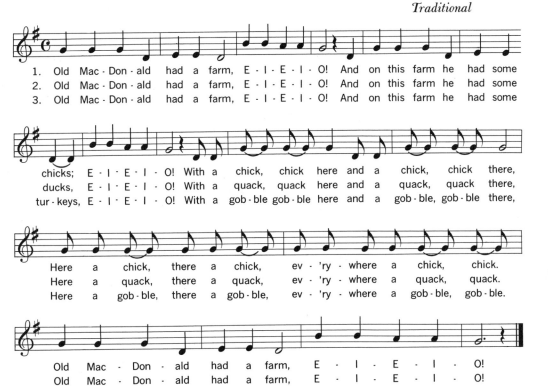

1. Old Mac - Don - ald had a farm, E - I - E - I - O! And on this farm he had some
2. Old Mac - Don - ald had a farm, E - I - E - I - O! And on this farm he had some
3. Old Mac - Don - ald had a farm, E - I - E - I - O! And on this farm he had some

chicks; E - I - E - I - O! With a chick, chick here and a chick, chick there,
ducks, E - I - E - I - O! With a quack, quack here and a quack, quack there,
tur - keys, E - I - E - I - O! With a gob - ble gob - ble here and a gob - ble, gob - ble there,

Here a chick, there a chick, ev - 'ry - where a chick, chick.
Here a quack, there a quack, ev - 'ry - where a quack, quack.
Here a gob - ble, there a gob - ble, ev - 'ry - where a gob - ble, gob - ble.

Old Mac - Don - ald had a farm, E - I - E - I - O!
Old Mac - Don - ald had a farm, E - I - E - I - O!
Old Mac - Don - ald had a farm, E - I - E - I - O!

107

JOHN BROWN HAD A LITTLE INDIAN

Traditional

John Brown had a lit - tle In - dian, John Brown had a lit - tle In - dian,

John Brown had a lit - tle In - dian, One lit - tle In - dian boy.

One lit - tle, two lit - tle, three lit - tle In - dians,
Ten lit - tle, nine lit - tle, eight lit - tle In - dians,

Four lit - tle, five lit - tle, six lit - tle In - dians,
Sev'n lit - tle, six lit - tle, five lit - tle In - dians,

Sev'n lit - tle, eight lit - tle, nine lit - tle In - dians,
Four lit - tle, three lit - tle, two lit - tle In - dians,

Ten lit - tle In - dian boys.
One lit - tle In - dian boy.

AULD LANG SYNE[3]

Robert Burns   *Scotch Air*

Should auld ac - quain - tance be for - got And nev - er brought to mind, Should auld ac -

Refrain

quain - tance be for - got And days of auld lang syne? For auld lang syne, my dear,

For auld lang syne; We'll take a cup of kind - ness yet, For auld lang syne.

3.   This song is based on the pentatonic scale. See footnote on page 61.

SOFT, SOFT MUSIC IS STEALING

Traditional College Song

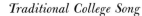
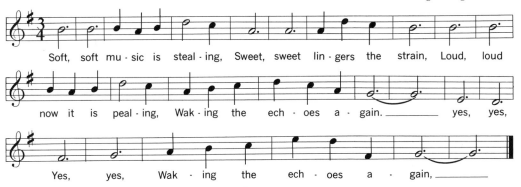

Soft, soft mu-sic is steal-ing, Sweet, sweet lin-gers the strain, Loud, loud

now it is peal-ing, Wak-ing the ech-oes a-gain. _____ yes, yes,

Yes, yes, Wak-ing the ech-oes a-gain, _____

DOWN IN THE VALLEY

Kentucky Mountain Ballad

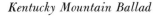
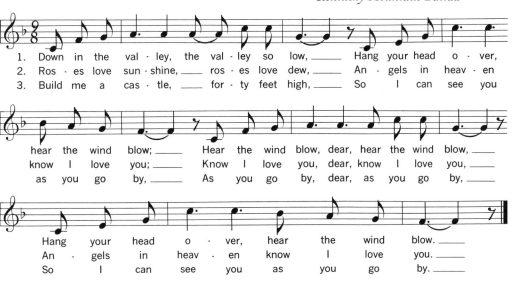

1. Down in the val-ley, the val-ley so low, _____ Hang your head o-ver,
2. Ros-es love sun-shine, _____ ros-es love dew, _____ An-gels in heav-en
3. Build me a cas-tle, _____ for-ty feet high, _____ So I can see you

hear the wind blow; _____ Hear the wind blow, dear, hear the wind blow, _____
know I love you; _____ Know I love you, dear, know I love you, _____
as you go by, _____ As you go by, dear, as you go by, _____

Hang your head o-ver, hear the wind blow. _____
An-gels in heav-en know I love you. _____
So I can see you as you go by. _____

String Instruments

Among classroom chordal instruments of the string family are the ukulele and Autoharp.[1] The ukulele is a small Hawaiian guitar with four strings and is easy to play. Each chord is indicated by four vertical lines representing the strings and small dots to show the positions of the fingers in relation to the frets (a series of ridges across the neck and fingerboard of the instrument).[2]

The Autoharp is an excellent chording instrument derived from the zither, an instrument of ancient origin. The Autoharp, however, has bars clearly marked for the different chords. Since the Autoharp is found extensively in elementary schools, it is the instrument selected for this textbook.

Keys and Chords of the Twelve-bar Autoharp[3]

The bars of this instrument play in the major keys of C, F, and G and in the minor keys of A and D. They form eight chords related to the key of C major, eight related to F major, six related to G major, and the three principal chords of A and D minor. Whereas chords can be indicated by name, letter, or number, they are shown only by letter on the Autoharp. However, you easily can change these into names and numbers. If, for instance, you are playing in the key of F major, the bar marked F is the *tonic,* or I, chord, the bar marked B♭ is the *subdominant,* or IV, chord, and C₇ is the *dominant seventh,* or V₇, chord.

Many songs in elementary school song textbooks show chords for the Autoharp. But if they do not, you can indicate the appropriate ones by following the directions given on page 105.

How to Play the Autoharp

Place the Autoharp on your lap, a desk, or a table. The long, flat side of the instrument should be next to you, with the right-hand corner somewhat closer to you than the left-hand corner. That is, the instrument should be at a slight angle. Press the desired chord bars firmly, one at a time, with the fingers of your left hand. Hold the chord bar down as you strum away from you across the strings with a felt or plastic pick held between the thumb and forefinger of your right hand. In this way, you strike the low tones (the long strings) of the chord first and move to the high tones (the short strings). You may strum at the right side of the bars or to the left (by crossing your right hand over the left), thus playing in the middle of the instrument. It obviously is easier to play to the right until you are familiar with the bars.

Patterns of Strumming

Depending on the song, you will use different patterns of strumming. Your stroke may be either long or short, light or heavy. Sometimes, if the same harmony is repeated throughout the measure, you will stroke the strings only once

---

1. "Autoharp" is the registered copyright trademark name of the manufacturer, Oscar Schmidt International, Inc., Garden State Rd., Union, N.J. Other chordal instruments are the guitar, Harmolin, and Guitaro.

2. See Appendix F (page 168) for names of instruction books for the ukulele.

3. The Autoharp is also made in smaller and larger sizes. The twelve-bar instrument is a practical and favorite size.

during the measure; or you may strum with each measure accent, or possibly only on the strong accent; or you may strum the rhythmic pattern. A felt pick gives a softer tone than a plastic one, but pressure and place of strumming affect both loudness and quality of tone. Again it is emphasized that you must always hold the bar down steadily as you stroke the strings; otherwise, the chord will be a blur of sound.

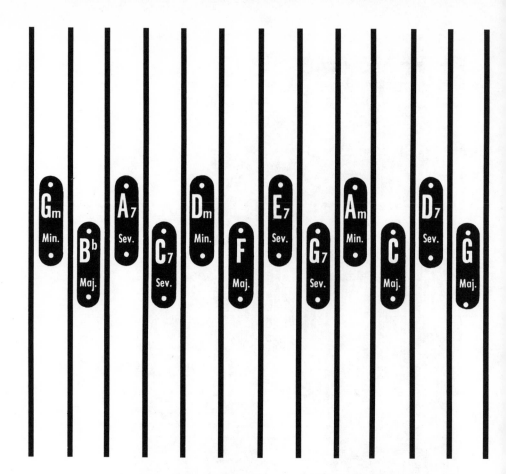

Care of the Autoharp

It is important that the instrument always be in tune. The length of time it stays so depends to a great extent on how carefully you treat it. You should, for example, never place it where it is extremely hot or extremely cold or where it is too damp or too dry.

To tune the Autoharp, apply a peg to each string and gently turn it until the tone matches the corresponding tone of a well-tuned piano. Begin tuning with the long, heavy strings, one at a time, and work to the short, lighter ones. Check your tuning by octaves and by chords.[4]

Assignment

1. Press different bars of the Autoharp and strum in different places to become familiar with the instrument and to determine where you get the best quality of tone.

2. Make a chart of the chord bars. Make the chart large enough so that you can practice finding the different chords easily.

3. Press the chord bars and strum:

C, F, G, G_7, C; F, C, B♭, C_7, F; G, C, D_7, G; A minor, D minor, E_7, A minor; D minor, G minor, A_7, D minor

4. The manual of instructions provided with the instrument gives you explicit directions regarding the care and tuning.

112

4. After you sing the following songs, play them with the chords as indicated. Experiment with different patterns of strumming.

JACOB'S LADDER

Spiritual

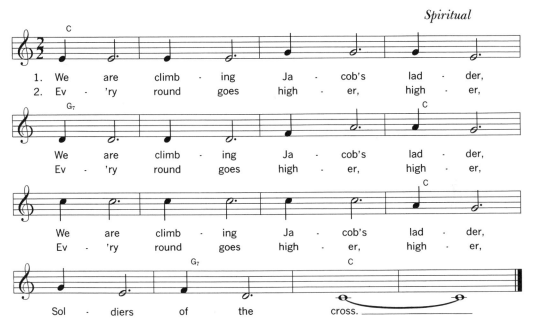

1. We are climb - ing Ja - cob's lad - der,
2. Ev - 'ry round goes high - er, high - er,

We are climb - ing Ja - cob's lad - der,
Ev - 'ry round goes high - er, high - er,

We are climb - ing Ja - cob's lad - der,
Ev - 'ry round goes high - er, high - er,

Sol - diers of the cross. _____

3. We are climbing higher, higher . . . .

4. We are climbing Jacob's ladder . . . .

FOR HE'S A JOLLY GOOD FELLOW

Old Song

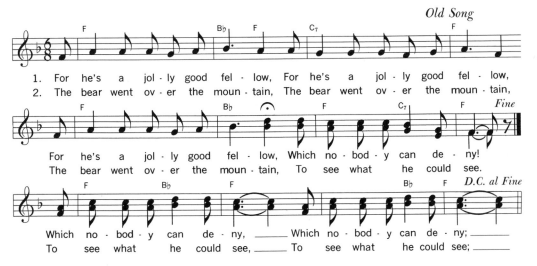

1. For he's a jol - ly good fel - low, For he's a jol - ly good fel - low,
2. The bear went ov - er the moun - tain, The bear went ov - er the moun - tain,

For he's a jol - ly good fel - low, Which no - bod - y can de - ny!
The bear went ov - er the moun - tain, To see what he could see.

Which no - bod - y can de - ny, _____ Which no - bod - y can de - ny; _____
To see what he could see, _____ To see what he could see; _____

3. The other side of the mountain
Was all that he could see.

4. My mother and father were Irish,
And I am Irish, too.

5. We bought a peck of potatoes,
For they were Irish, too.

6. We won't go home 'till morning,
Till daylight doth appear.

113

CLEMENTINE

American Folk Song

1. In a cav-ern, in a can-yon, Ex-ca-vat-ting for a
2. Light she was and like a fair-y, And her shoes were num-ber

mine, Dwelt a min-er, for-ty-nin-er, And his daugh-ter, Clem-en-tine.
nine, Her-ring box-es with-out tops-es, San-dals were for Clem-en-tine.

Refrain

O my dar-ling, O my dar-ling, O my dar-ling Clem-en-

tine! You are lost and gone for-ev-er; Dread-ful sor-ry, Clem-en-tine.

3. Drove she ducklings to the water
   Ev'ry morning just at nine;
   Hit her foot against a splinter,
   Fell into the foaming brine.

4. Then the miner, forty-niner,
   Soon began to peak and pine;
   Thought he ought to join his daughter;
   Now he's with his Clementine.

I'VE BEEN WORKING ON THE RAILROAD

American Work Song

I've been work-ing on the rail-road All the live-long day;

I've been work-ing on the rail-road to pass the time a-way.

Don't you hear the whis-tle blow-ing? Rise up so ear-ly in the

morn. Don't you hear the cap-tain shout-ing: "Di-nah, blow your horn!"

114

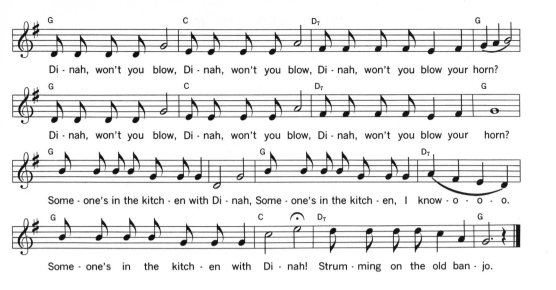

Di - nah, won't you blow, Di - nah, won't you blow, Di - nah, won't you blow your horn?

Di - nah, won't you blow, Di - nah, won't you blow, Di - nah, won't you blow your   horn?

Some - one's in the kitch - en with Di - nah, Some - one's in the kitch - en, I   know - o - o - o.

Some - one's in   the   kitch - en   with   Di - nah!   Strum - ming on the old ban - jo.

A WEE MAN IN THE WOODS

From Hansel and Gretel, by Humperdinck

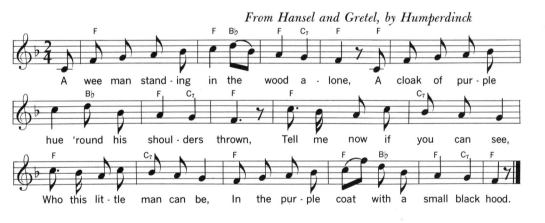

A   wee man stand - ing   in the   wood a - lone,   A   cloak   of   pur - ple

hue 'round his   shoul - ders   thrown,   Tell   me   now   if   you   can   see,

Who this lit - tle   man can be,   In   the   pur - ple   coat   with a   small black hood.

EZEKIEL SAW THE WHEEL

Negro Spiritual

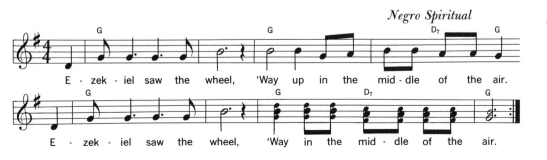

E - zek - iel saw the   wheel,   'Way   up   in   the   mid - dle   of   the air.

E - zek - iel   saw   the   wheel,   'Way   in   the   mid - dle   of   the   air.

COMIN' THRO' THE RYE

Robert Burns

Scotch Air

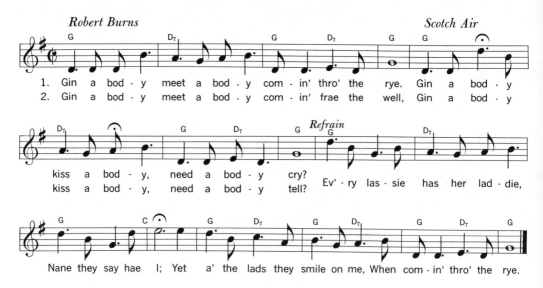

1. Gin a bod - y meet a bod - y com - in' thro' the rye. Gin a bod - y
2. Gin a bod - y meet a bod - y com - in' frae the well, Gin a bod - y

kiss a bod - y, need a bod - y cry?
kiss a bod - y, need a bod - y tell?

Refrain

Ev' - ry las - sie has her lad - die,

Nane they say hae I; Yet a' the lads they smile on me, When com - in' thro' the rye.

THE TAILOR AND THE MOUSE

English Folk Song

With a Lilt

1. There was a tai - lor had a mouse;
2. The tai - lor tho't the mouse was ill; Hi - did - dle un - kum fee - dle!
3. And so he gave him cat - nip tea;

They lived to - geth - er in one house;
Be - cause he took an a - gue chill; Hi - did - dle un - kum fee - dle!
Un - til a heart - y mouse was he;

Refrain

Hi - did - dle un - kum tar - um, tan - tum! Thro' the town of Ram - say;

116

Hi - did - dle un - kum, o - ver the lea, Hi - did - dle un - kum fee - dle!

CHANUKAH, OH CHANUKAH

Alice Firgau

Hasidic Folk Song

'Tis the week of Cha - nu - kah, Good cheer it is bring - ing. This
hol - i - day we cel - e - brate in danc - ing and sing - ing.

Gath - er 'round to - geth - er, the ho - ra we'll do; Then join in a song that our

fore - fa - thers knew. But hush now and come now, The can - dles we light one by one.

Then hear the sto - ry of God and His glo - ry And how pre - cious free - dom was won.

From *Making Music Your Own*, Book Six. Copyright 1965, Silver Burdett Company, Morristown., N.J. Used by permission.

5. What chords would you use in the following songs? Play them as you sing the songs. Did you select the right chords?

SEE-SAW, MARGERY DAW

Mother Goose

J. W. Elliott

See - saw, Mar - ger - y Daw, Jack shall have a new mas - ter;

He shall have but a pen - ny a day Be - cause he won't work an - y fas - ter.

117

BILLY BOY

Mountain Folk Song

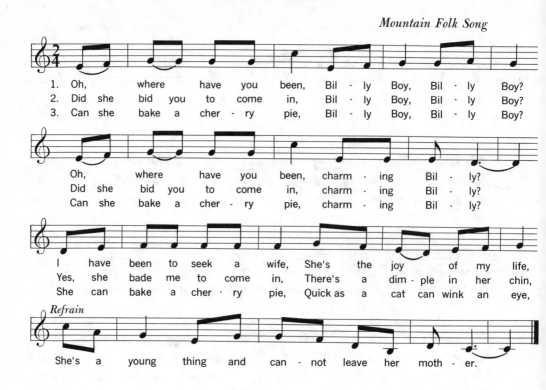

1. Oh, where have you been, Bil - ly Boy, Bil - ly Boy?
2. Did she bid you to come in, Bil - ly Boy, Bil - ly Boy?
3. Can she bake a cher - ry pie, Bil - ly Boy, Bil - ly Boy?

Oh, where have you been, charm - ing Bil - ly?
Did she bid you to come in, charm - ing Bil - ly?
Can she bake a cher - ry pie, charm - ing Bil - ly?

I have been to seek a wife, She's the joy of my life,
Yes, she bade me to come in, There's a dim - ple in her chin,
She can bake a cher - ry pie, Quick as a cat can wink an eye,

Refrain

She's a young thing and can - not leave her moth - er.

SOME FOLKS

Stephen C. Foster

Briskly

1. Some folks like to sigh,
2. Some folks fear to smile, Some folks do, some folks do;
3. Some folks get gray hairs,

Some folks long to die,
Oth - ers laugh through guile, But that's not me or you.
Brood - ing o'er their cares,

Refrain

Long live the mer - ry, mer - ry heart That laughs by night and

day Like the Queen of Mirth, No mat - ter what some folks say.

118

HOME ON THE RANGE

Cowboy Song

Oh, give me a home where the buf - fa - lo roam, where the deer and the an - te - lope play,

Where sel - dom is heard a dis - cour - ag - ing word, and the skies are not cloud - y all day.

Home, home on the range, where the deer and the an - te - lope play,

Where sel - dom is heard a dis - cour - ag - ing word, and the skies are not cloud - y all day.

6. Practice these songs on the piano with chordal accompaniment.

7. Select songs in preceding chapters to play on the Autoharp.[5]

5. For additional information and songs see *The Many Ways to Play the Autoharp,* Vols. I and II, Oscar Schmidt International, Inc., Union, N.J., 1966.

Sight singing is the ability to hear music mentally from its notation and then to reproduce it audibly by means of the voice. It is a valuable musical skill and an important aspect of musicianship.

Up to now you have had opportunities to sing by note, learn theoretical facts, and deal with the musical score through the use of songs, the piano, song bells, and the Autoharp. This foundation of skills and knowledge is necessary before eye, ear, and voice can work well together in sight singing. As with any other skill, reading music at sight requires consistent practice, and you will learn to read fluently and pleasurably if you read extensively.

suggestions

1. Read the words to get the meaning.
2. Notice dynamic and tempo markings.
3. Study the form of the song to find phrases that are alike and those that are different.
4. Observe the meter signature and determine the basic beats in each measure.
5. Scan the words rhythmically to find recurring rhythmic patterns.
6. Name the key and mode and the beginning and ending tones.
7. Find scale and chordal sequences. Look also for repeated intervals.
8. Get the exact pitch of the scale tone of the song from the piano, song bells, or a pitch pipe.[1] Establish the tonality of the song by singing the tones of the tonic chord (1-3-5-3-1, or *do-mi-sol-mi-do*) or part of the scale (1-2-3-4-5-4-3-2-1, or *do-re-mi-fa-sol-fa-mi-re-do*). Then sing the beginning tone of the song.
9. Establish the tempo at which you wish to sing the song. After you start singing the song, keep the rhythm moving.
10. Sing the song with syllables or numbers (or both) and with the words. If any interval presents difficulty, isolate it and sing the intervening notes. Then sing the interval and *think* the intervening tones.

Assignment

With the preceding suggestions in mind, read the following songs.

BLOW THE WINDS SOUTHERLY

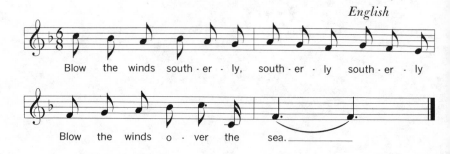

English

Blow the winds south-er-ly, south-er-ly south-er-ly

Blow the winds o-ver the sea.

---

1. In the chromatic pitch pipe, the names of the pitches are indicated above the corresponding holes. To get the desired pitch, round the lips (as when whistling) and gently and steadily blow into the proper hole.

sight singing

14

ST. PAUL'S STEEPLE

English Folk Song

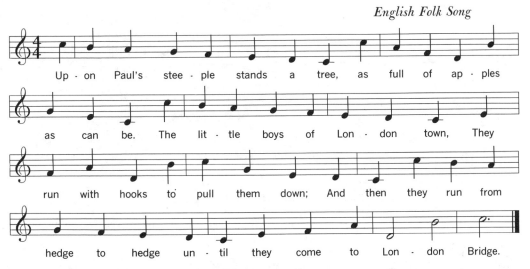

Up-on Paul's stee-ple stands a tree, as full of ap-ples as can be. The lit-tle boys of Lon-don town, They run with hooks to pull them down; And then they run from hedge to hedge un-til they come to Lon-don Bridge.

From *New Music Horizons,* Book Five. Copyright 1946, 1953, Silver Burdett Company, Morristown, N.J. Used by permission.

LITTLE MOHEE

Mountain Song

I once was a stran-ger and far from my home, And in a strange coun-try 'way o-ver the foam; As I sat a-wait-ing the time for to pass, I saw com-ing near me such a fair In-dian lass.

BLOW THE MAN DOWN

American Sailor Chantey

121

Come, all you young fel-lows that fol-low the sea, With a yeo-ho! We'll blow the man down! And please pay at-ten-tion and lis-ten to me. Give us some time to blow the man down.

THE GALWAY PIPER

Irish Folk Song

Con Spirito

Ev - 'ry per - son in the na - tion, Of a great or hum - ble sta - tion,

Holds in high - est es - ti - ma - tion Pip - ing Tim of Gal - way;

Loud - ly he can play or low, He can move you fast or slow,

Touch your heart or stir your toe, Pip - ing Tim of Gal - way.

HAUL AWAY, JOE

Sea Chantey

1. A - way, haul a - way, Come haul a - way - to geth - er;
2. A - way, haul a - way, I'll sing to you of Nan - cy;

A - way, haul a - way, Haul a - way, Joe.

A - way, haul a - way, We'll haul for fin - er weath - er;
A - way, haul a - way, She's just my style and fan - cy;

A - way, haul a - way, We'll haul a - way, Joe.

PASSING BY

Anonymous Poem from Thomas Ford's
Music of Sundry Kinds (1607)

Edward Purcell

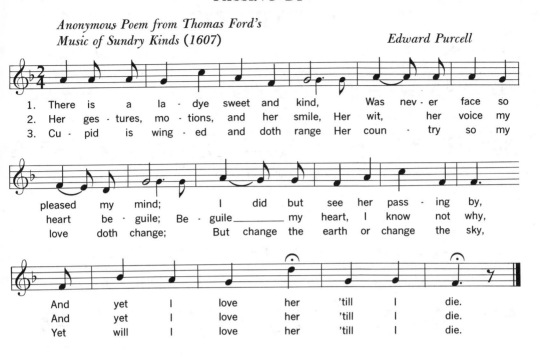

1. There is a la - dye sweet and kind, Was nev - er face so
2. Her ges - tures, mo - tions, and her smile, Her wit, her voice my
3. Cu - pid is wing - ed and doth range Her coun - try so my

pleased my mind; I did but see her pass - ing by,
heart be - guile; Be - guile_____ my heart, I know not why,
love doth change; But change the earth or change the sky,

And yet I love her 'till I die.
And yet I love her 'till I die.
Yet will I love her 'till I die.

I HAD A LITTLE NUT TREE

Traditional

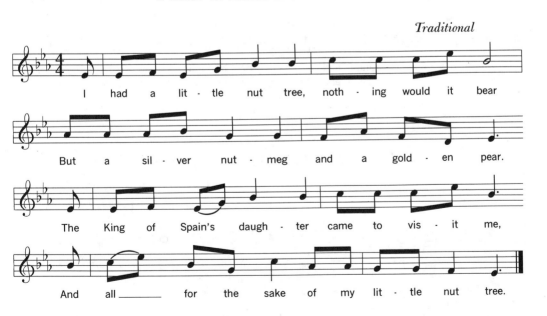

I had a lit - tle nut tree, noth - ing would it bear

But a sil - ver nut - meg and a gold - en pear.

The King of Spain's daugh - ter came to vis - it me,

123

And all _____ for the sake of my lit - tle nut tree.

LULLY, LULLAY
(COVENTRY CAROL)

Traditional English Carol

Lul - ly, lul - lay, thou lit - tle ti - ny child, By, by, lul - ly, lul - lay. ____

Lul - lay, thou lit - tle ti - ny child, By, by, lul - ly, lul - lay. ____

WHEN THAT I WAS A TINY BOY

William Shakespeare (1564–1616)   *Joseph Vernon (1737–1782)*

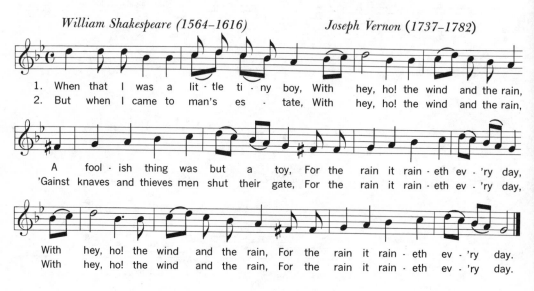

1. When that I was a lit - tle ti - ny boy, With hey, ho! the wind and the rain,
2. But when I came to man's es - tate, With hey, ho! the wind and the rain,

A fool - ish thing was but a toy, For the rain it rain - eth ev - 'ry day,
'Gainst knaves and thieves men shut their gate, For the rain it rain - eth ev - 'ry day,

With hey, ho! the wind and the rain, For the rain it rain - eth ev - 'ry day.
With hey, ho! the wind and the rain, For the rain it rain - eth ev - 'ry day.

NOW IS THE MONTH OF MAYING

Madrigal by Thomas Morley
(1537–1603)

Vivace

124

1. Now is the month of may - ing, When mer - ry lads are play - ing,
2. The spring, clad all in glad - ness, Doth laugh at win - ter's sad - ness,
3. Fye, then, why sit we mus - ing, Sweet youth's de - lights re - fus - ing?

Fa la la la la la la la la, Fa la la la la la la.

Each with his bon-ny lass, A danc-ing on the grass,
And to the bag-pipe's sound, The nymphs tread out their ground,
Say, dain-ty nymphs, and speak, Shall we play bar-ley break?

Fa la la la la, fa la la la la la la la la la la la.

BESIDE THY CRADLE HERE I STAND*

From Christmas Oratorio,
by Johann Sebastian Bach

In Choral Style

Be-side Thy cra-dle here I stand, O Thou that ev-er liv-est,

And bring Thee with a will-ing hand The ver-y gifts Thou giv-est.

Ac-cept me; 'tis my mind and heart, My soul, my strength, my

ev-'ry part, That Thou from me re-quir-est.

GUARDIAN ANGELS*

Robert Schumann; Opus 79, No. 21

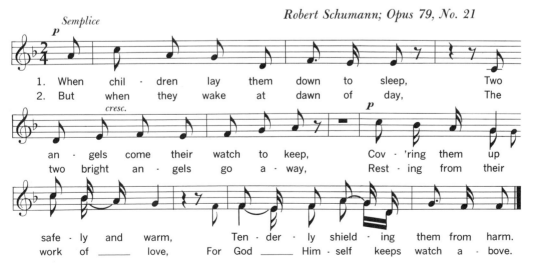

Semplice
p

1. When chil-dren lay them down to sleep, Two
2. But when they wake at dawn of day, The

cresc.   p

an-gels come their watch to keep, Cov-'ring them up
two bright an-gels go a-way, Rest-ing from their

safe-ly and warm, Ten-der-ly shield-ing them from harm.
work of ____ love, For God ____ Him-self keeps watch a-bove.

125

WANDERING*

Wihelm Müller   *Franz Schubert*

To wan-der is the mil-ler's joy, To wan-der.

He must a wretch-ed mil-ler be Who nev-er cares the

world to see, To wan-der, to wan-der, to wan-der, to wan-der.

ROCK OF AGES

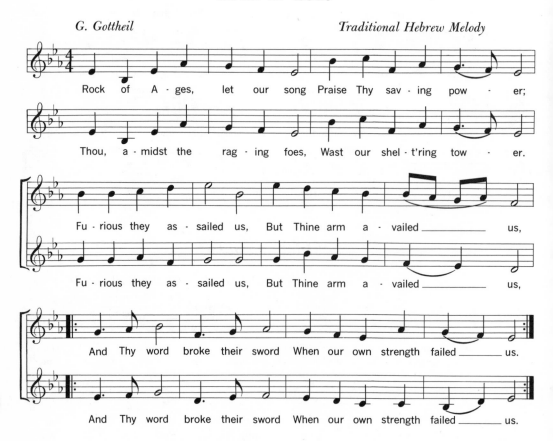

G. Gottheil   *Traditional Hebrew Melody*

Rock of A-ges, let our song Praise Thy sav-ing pow - er;

Thou, a-midst the rag-ing foes, Wast our shel-t'ring tow - er.

Fu-rious they as-sailed us, But Thine arm a-vailed _____ us,

Fu-rious they as-sailed us, But Thine arm a-vailed _____ us,

And Thy word broke their sword When our own strength failed _____ us.

And Thy word broke their sword When our own strength failed _____ us.

126

Other songs for sight reading can be found in elementary song textbooks. See
Appendix F (page 168).

Embellishing Tones

Sharps (♯, 𝄪), flats (♭, ♭♭), and naturals (♮) not only form scales but also contribute certain musical effects within a composition. When they are used in a transitory way, they are termed "accidentals" or "embellishing tones." Their effect carries throughout the measure in which they occur, ending at the bar line unless the note so marked is tied to a note on the same degree in the next measure.

Accidentals apply not only to the note before which they appear but to all notes of the same pitch within the same octave.

example of accidentals in a melody

I HEARD THE BELLS

Henry W. Longfellow   John B. Calkin

1. I heard the bells on Christ - mas day Their
2. I thought how, as the day had come, The

old, fa - mil - iar car - ols play, And wild and sweet the
bel - fries of all Chris - ten - dom Had rolled a - long the un-

words re - peat Of peace on earth, good will to men.
brok - en song Of peace on earth, good will to men.

CRADLE SONG

Wolfgang Amadeus Mozart

Sleep, O my ba · by, and rest; Birds are a · sleep in their nest. Gar · den and mead · ow are still; Bees hum no more by the rill. In thro' the win · dow so bright, Shines the moon sil · ver · y light. Nes · tle your head on my breast; Sleep, O my ba · by, and rest. O sleep, _____ O sleep.

Change of Key within a Song

Sometimes a song does not remain in the same key throughout but, by the use of accidentals, moves from one key to another. This serves to bring out the meaning of the words and to increase and maintain musical interest. Change of keys within a song is known as "modulation." As a rule, the modulation is to nearly related keys, that is, keys whose signature does not differ by more than one or two sharps or flats.[1] Some songs not only change key but change the mode as well. Observe this in the song "Courage," where Schubert shifts from minor to major in accordance with the changing mood of the words.

1. Accidentals to bring about modulation do not always occur in the melody but may be found in the harmony or accompaniment.

COURAGE[2]

Wilhelm Müller

Allegro Assai, Energico

Franz Schubert

1. When the snow ____ flies in my face, Off I gai - ly ____ brush it.
2. Lis - ten not ____ when it com - plains, Turn a - way my hear - ing;

Would my heart its troubles
Will not feel its cares and

2. This song is one that appears in the "Winter Journey" (*Winterreise*), a cycle of twenty-four songs. It describes the journey of a young man and expresses the emotions of joy and depression experienced by him.

129

speak; Loud I sing to hush it.
pains, Fools are prone to fear - ing.

f

Mer - ri - ly I trudge a - long, 'Gainst the wind and weath - er;

mf

Trus - ty staff and cheer - ful song, On we'll go to -

f

mf

geth - er!   Mer - ri - ly I   trudge a - long,

'Gainst the wind and weath - er!   Trus - ty staff and

cheer - ful song, On we'll go to - geth - er.

131

In most simple songs, the change of key is brief (usually only a cadence in the new key), and then the song returns to the original key, as for example, in "America, the Beautiful."

AMERICA, THE BEAUTIFUL*

Katharine Lee Bates   Samuel A. Ward

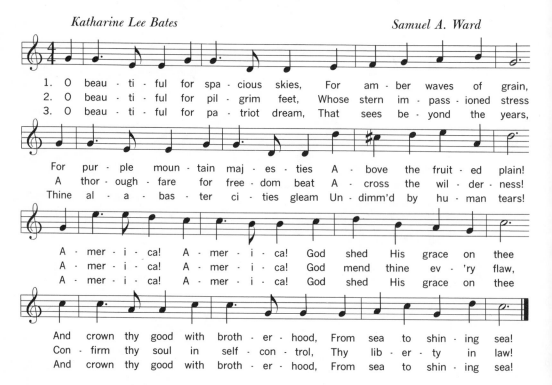

1. O beau - ti - ful for spa - cious skies, For am - ber waves of grain,
2. O beau - ti - ful for pil - grim feet, Whose stern im - pass - ioned stress
3. O beau - ti - ful for pa - triot dream, That sees be - yond the years,

For pur - ple moun - tain maj - es - ties A - bove the fruit - ed plain!
A thor - ough - fare for free - dom beat A - cross the wil - der - ness!
Thine al - a - bas - ter ci - ties gleam Un - dimm'd by hu - man tears!

A - mer - i - ca! A - mer - i - ca! God shed His grace on thee
A - mer - i - ca! A - mer - i - ca! God mend thine ev - 'ry flaw,
A - mer - i - ca! A - mer - i - ca! God shed His grace on thee

And crown thy good with broth - er - hood, From sea to shin - ing sea!
Con - firm thy soul in self - con - trol, Thy lib - er - ty in law!
And crown thy good with broth - er - hood, From sea to shin - ing sea!

Assignment

1. Explain accidentals and modulation and give specific illustrations by writing original exercises.

2. **a** Sing "America, the Beautiful" and point out just where modulation takes place.

  b Name the beginning and ending keys and the key to which the song modulates.

  c How was modulation brought about; that is, what accidental is used and where? What is the relationship of the modulatory tone to the original and the modulating key?

3. Review songs in preceding chapters to observe the use of chromatics *within* the song. Cite two or three examples of each of the following: where chromatics were used to embellish the melody, where they were used to bring about modulation, and where they were used to form the minor mode.

4. After singing the following songs, determine whether chromatics bring about modulation or whether they are used merely as accidentals. If modulation occurs, name the original and ending keys and the modulating key, and tell just where and how modulation is brought about.

5. Practice singing three or four of these songs with *sol-fa* syllables, scale numbers, and degree letter names.

6. Play these songs on the piano and song bells.

DECK THE HALL*

Welsh Carol

1. { Deck the hall with boughs of hol - ly,
   { 'Tis the sea - son to be jol - ly,
2. { See the blaz - ing Yule be - fore us,
   { Strike the harp and join the cho - rus,

Fa la la la la la la la la.

Don we now our gay ap - par - el,
Fol - low me in mer - ry meas - ure,

Fa la la la la la la la la.

Troll the an - cient Yule - tide car - ol,
While I tell of Yule - tide treas - ure,

Fa la la la la la la la la.

SUMMER DAYS

Franz Joseph Haydn

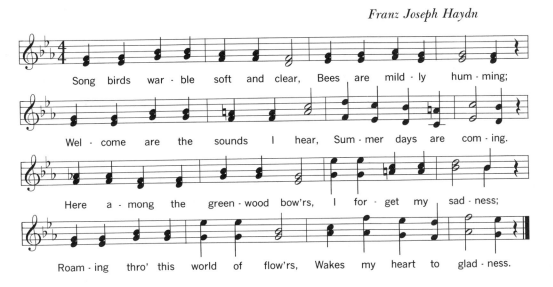

Song birds war - ble soft and clear, Bees are mild - ly hum - ming;

Wel - come are the sounds I hear, Sum - mer days are com - ing.

Here a - mong the green - wood bow'rs, I for - get my sad - ness;

Roam - ing thro' this world of flow'rs, Wakes my heart to glad - ness.

133

LONGING FOR SPRING*

Wolfgang Amadeus Mozart

1. Come, love-ly May, and make thou The trees once more be green; Once
2. Ah, would it were but mild-er And green-er round our home; Come,

more a-long the brook-side Let vi-o-lets be seen. I
love-ly May, we chil-dren En-treat of thee to come. O

long with ea-ger long-ing for vi-o-lets to grow; Ah,
come, all wood and mea-dow, with vi-o-lets' per-fume; Bid

love-ly May, how glad-ly A-walk-ing I would go.
night-in-gale and cuck-oo Their wel-come notes re-sume.

THE SWALLOW

Words Adapted by Hervey White

Mexican Folk Song

Where are you go-ing, lone-ly lit-tle swal - low? Your wings are

wear-y, you have flown so far.____ I, too, am lone-ly; would that I might

fol-low Your flight to where my friends and loved ones are._____ This bleak, lone

land,____ it can-not lift my sor-row; my bar-ren

heart is dead and dry with pain. Come back, dear bird, come back a-gain to-

mor-row; Tell me of those I ne'er shall see a-gain.____

TIT WILLOW*

W. S. Gilbert

*From The Mikado,
by Sir Arthur Sullivan*

1. On a tree by a riv - er a lit - tle tom - tit Sang
2. He slapp'd at his chest as he sat on the bough, Sing - ing
3. Now I feel just as sure as I'm sure that my name Is - n't

1. "Wil - low, tit - wil - low, tit - wil - low." And I
2. "Wil - low, tit - wil - low, tit - wil - low." And a
3. wil - low, tit - wil - low, tit - wil - low, That 'twas

1. said to him, "Dick - y - bird, why do you sit, Sing - ing
2. cold per - spi - ra - tion be - span - gled his brow, "Oh,
3. blight - ed af - fec - tion that made him ex - claim, "Oh,

1. wil - low, tit - wil - low, tit - wil - low?" Is it
2. wil - low, tit - wil - low, tit - wil - low." He
3. wil - low, tit - wil - low, tit - wil - low." And if

1. weak - ness of in - tel - lect, bir - die," I cried, "Or a
2. sobb'd, and he sigh'd, And a gur - gle he gave; Then he
3. you re - main cal - lous and ob - du - rate, I shall

1. rath - er tough worm in your lit - tle in - side?" With a
2. plung'd him - self in - to the bil - low - y wave, And an
3. per - ish as he did, and you will know why; Though I

1. shake of his poor lit - tle head, he re - plied, "Oh,
2. ech - o a - rose from the su - i - cide's grave, "Oh,
3. prob - a - bly shall not ex - claim as I die, "Oh,

1. will - low, tit - wil - low, tit - wil - low."
2. wil - low, tit - wil - low, tit - wil - low."
3. wil - low, tit - wil - low, tit - wil - low."

135

THE FIRST PRIMROSE*

J. Paulsen

Edvard Hagerup Grieg

Allegretto dolcissimo

Oh, take, thou love - ly child of Spring, This Spring's first ten - der

flow - er; Des - pise it not that la - ter on, Fair

ro - ses June will show - er. The sum - mer has its

gol - den charm, In au - tumn hearts are gay, _____ But

poco rit.

Spring is love - li - er than all, The time of love and

pp a tempo

play. _____ For thee and me, O dear - est maid, The

mf

light of Spring is glow - ing; Then take the flow'r and

dim. e poco rit. *p*

rap - ture yield, Thy heart on me be - stow - ing.

Definition and Purpose

Just as you can sing or play a scale beginning on any pitch, so you can change a song into a different key from the one in which it is written providing you keep the whole and half steps the same. Placing a composition into a lower or higher key is called "transposition." It is an important technique when teaching children since you frequently will need to shift the pitch of a song so that children can sing it easily and accurately. Sometimes you will need to change the key of a song in order to play it on a particular classroom instrument, such as the Autoharp.

How to Transpose

After tonality is established, it is a simple matter to sing a melody in different keys. But to write it or transpose it instrumentally is more complicated. However, if you know the exact positions of the notes in the scale, you can place their numbers near them and make the transposition to higher or lower keys without difficulty.

example

LONDON BRIDGE

Singing Game

THE CUCKOO

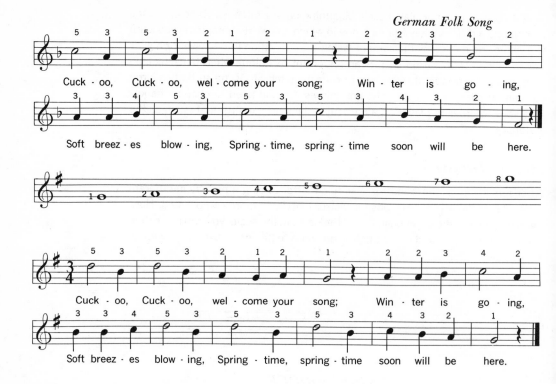

Cuck - oo, Cuck - oo, wel - come your song; Win - ter is go - ing,

Soft breez - es blow - ing, Spring - time, spring - time soon will be here.

Cuck - oo, Cuck - oo, wel - come your song; Win - ter is go - ing,

Soft breez - es blow - ing, Spring - time, spring - time soon will be here.

Assignment

1. Sing and play this song in the key of F, as written; then write and play it in the key of G.

LONG, LONG AGO

Thomas H. Bayly

Tell me the tales that to me were so dear, Long, long a - go, Long, long a - go;

Sing me the songs I de - light - ed to hear, Long, long a - go, long a - go.

2. Sing and play "America" in the key of G, as written (page 12); then write and play it in the key of F.

3. Play and sing this song in the key of G, as written; then play and sing it in the key of F.

WHEN I WAS A LADY

English Singing Game

When I was a la-dy, a la-dy, a la-dy, And when I was a

la-dy, a la-dy was I; And this way and that way, And

this way and that way, And when I was a la-dy, a la-dy was I.

4. Transpose the following songs into appropriate keys for the Autoharp.[1]
Write the chords with markings for each measure.

example

BATTLE HYMN OF THE REPUBLIC

Bb (or I Chord)   Bb

Mine eyes have seen the glo - ry of the com - ing of the Lord,

Transposed to Key of C

Mine eyes have seen the glo - ry of the com - ing of the Lord,

C (or I Chord)   C

1. The twelve-bar instrument plays in the major keys of C, F, and G and the minor keys of A and
D (refer to page 110).

139

LITTLE JACK HORNER

Nursery Rhyme

J. W. Elliott

Lit - tle Jack Hor - ner sat in a cor - ner, Eat - ing his Christ - mas pie; _____

He put in his thumb and pulled out a plum, And said, "What a good boy am I!" ___

EARLY ONE MORNING

Old English Song

Ear - ly one morn - ing, just as the sun was ris - ing,

I heard a maid sing in the val - ley so low:

"Oh! don't de - ceive me, Oh! nev - er leave me.

How could you treat a poor maid - en so?"

"Lullaby" by Brahms (page 23)
"She'll Be Coming 'Round the Mountain" (page 15)
"My Bonnie" (page 79)

140

One of the best ways to test your musical knowledge and skills is to use notation in composing an original song. Some of you may do this with comparative ease. Others, however, may find it difficult. But great composers also labored over their compositions. Beethoven and Brahms sometimes took years perfecting their work. On the other hand, Mozart and Schubert wrote easily, skillfully, and quickly. In either event, you have to start with a musical idea. In the case of songs, this may come from the poem you select to set to music. You may have to try different plans before you are satisfied that your song is musically interesting.

Composed by a child of nine years of age

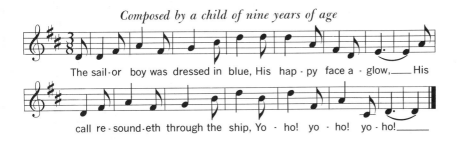

The sail-or boy was dressed in blue, His hap-py face a-glow,____ His call re-sound-eth through the ship, Yo-ho! yo-ho! yo-ho!____

Composed by a child of eight years of age

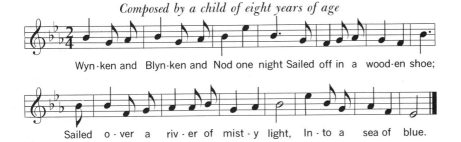

Wyn-ken and Blyn-ken and Nod one night Sailed off in a wood-en shoe; Sailed o-ver a riv-er of mist-y light, In-to a sea of blue.

Composed by a child of six years of age

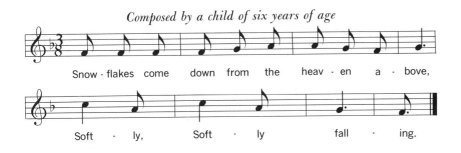

Snow-flakes come down from the heav-en a-bove, Soft-ly, Soft-ly fall-ing.

The children experimented with the above songs by singing and playing them on the bells and piano until each child was satisfied with his composition. Then the children asked their teacher to record the songs in notation.

Completion of Phrases

An easy and helpful approach to song composition is to complete the phrases of melodies. This probably will be done differently by different individuals.

original music 17

first (antecedent) phrase

Sleep, O sleep! While breez - es so soft - ly are blow - ing;

second (consequent) phrase

Example 1

Sleep, O sleep! While stream - lets so gent - ly are flow - ing.

Example 2

Sleep, O sleep! _____ While stream - lets so gent - ly are flow - ing.

Suggestions on Composing a Song

The first step in composing a song is to select or write a short, rhythmical poem. Read it thoughtfully to yourself and then out loud. Mark the stressed words and syllables and show the rhythmic pattern by use of long and short lines. Write the words under the staff. Decide on the meter signature and insert the bar lines in the proper places. The melody should express the mood of the poem, and it should be in an appropriate mode and key. Range of voice and form (unity, variety, and balance of phrases) are important. The accompaniment should be in keeping with the words and should add to the musical interest and meaning of the song. Tempo and dynamic markings should be added to indicate how the song is to be interpreted.

The Evening Star

142

Robert Schumann, a famous composer of the nineteenth century (1810–1856), set these simple verses to music in a felicitous way.

THE EVENING STAR

Robert Schumann; Opus 79, No. 1

1. O beau - ti - ful star, So ra - diant a - far, How dear - ly I love you Though dis - tant you are.
2. How bright - ly that eye, That spar - kles on high, Is gaz - ing and smil - ing On me from the sky.

Assignment

1. Complete the following phrases. Notice that the words determine the rhythm and the measure grouping.

Lit - tle white snow - drop, just wak - ing up, Vi - o - let, dai - sy, and sweet but - ter - cup; Un - der the leaves and the ice and the snow, Wait - ing, wait - ing, wait - ing to grow.

Hush - a - by, don't you cry, Go to sleep, my lit - tle ba - by;

When you wake, you shall have All the pret - ty lit - tle hors - es,

Blacks and bays, dap - ples and grays, Coach and six lit - tle hors - es;

Hush - a - by, don't you cry, Go to sleep, my lit - tle ba - by.

2. Set the words of the Schumann song to original music. If you prefer, select another poem. The following are examples of suitable poems:

Indian Lullaby

Rockaby, my little owlet,
    In thy mossy, swaying nest,
With thy little woodland brothers,
    Close thine eyes and take thy rest.
To whoo, to whoo, to whoo, to whoo.
       Henry Wadsworth Longfellow

Little White Feathers

Little white feathers filling the air,
    Little white feathers, how came you there?
We came from the storm winds sailing on high,
    They're shaking their white wings up in the sky.
       Eleanor Smith

Who Has Seen the Wind

Who has seen the wind?
    Neither I nor you,
But when the leaves hang trembling,
    The wind is passing through.

Who has seen the wind?
    Neither you nor I,
But when the trees bow down their heads,
    The wind is passing by.
       Christina Rossetti

The Swing

How do you like to go up in a swing,
    Up in the air so blue?
Oh, I do think it the pleasantest thing,
    Ever a child can do!

Up in the air and over the wall,
    'Till I can see so wide
Rivers and trees and cattle and all
    Over the countryside.

'Till I look down on the garden green,
    Down on the roof so brown,
Up in the air I go flying again,
    Up in the air and down!

Robert Louis Stevenson

Folk Songs

Songs which are characteristic of a people and of which the composers are unknown are termed "folk songs." They are an important part of a nation's musical heritage. Since for many years they were handed down orally from generation to generation, many valuable ones doubtless have been lost. But now, literally thousands have been collected, arranged, and put in permanent form.

As a folk tune is repeated through the years, singers unconsciously may make slight changes. After a time, these variations eventually bring about a tune essentially different from the original. This is the case in the English folk song "Barb'ra Allen." This old, romantic ballad with its many verses, was brought to America by our earliest settlers. A collector of folk songs is said to have found as many as ninety-eight versions in the state of Virginia. This is one of the most popular.

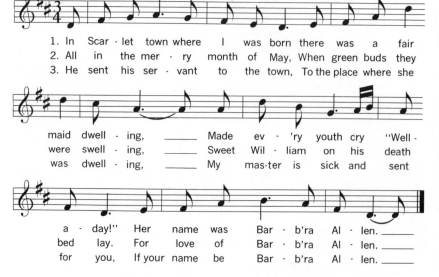

1. In Scar-let town where I was born there was a fair
   maid dwell-ing, _____ Made ev-'ry youth cry "Well-
   a-day!" Her name was Bar-b'ra Al-len. _____

2. All in the mer-ry month of May, When green buds they
   were swell-ing, _____ Sweet Wil-liam on his death
   bed lay. For love of Bar-b'ra Al-len. _____

3. He sent his ser-vant to the town, To the place where she
   was dwell-ing, _____ My mas-ter is sick and sent
   for you, If your name be Bar-b'ra Al-len. _____

4. Then slowly, slowly she got up,
   Then slowly she came nigh him,
   And all she said when there she came,
   "Young man, I think you're dying."

5. He turned his pale face to the wall
   And death was in him dwelling.
   "Adieu, adieu, to my friends all,
   Be kind to Barb'ra Allen.

Folk songs, along with the dances of a people, have inspired many great composers and have been woven by them into some of their most notable works. Brahms, for instance, loved the folk music of his country so much that he used it in both his instrumental and his choral works. Dvorak, the Czech composer, was greatly influenced by folk music. He is said to have listened always to the "voices of the people." However, he did not use tunes exactly as he heard them but employed them in an original way. Chopin's music showed the influence of Polish folk dances in the characteristic rhythms of his mazurkas and polonaises. In the ballet based on the story of "Billy, the Kid," the American composer Aaron Copland used songs of the cowboy wholly or in part. The music of Russian composers is closely linked with the folk music of their land. The simple Russian folk song "The Birch Tree" was used by Tchaikowsky as the main theme of the last movement of his Fourth Symphony.

THE BIRCH TREE

Russian Folk Song

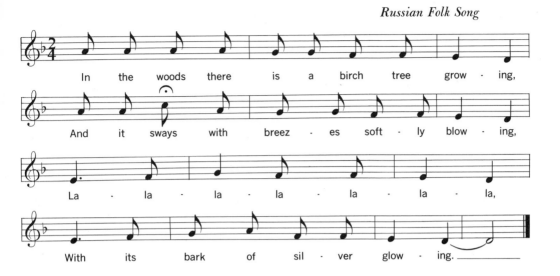

In the woods there is a birch tree grow - ing,

And it sways with breez - es soft - ly blow - ing,

La - la - la - la - la - la - la,

With its bark of sil - ver glow - ing. _____

Simple songs by known composers which express the spirit of a people and have through long use become a traditional part of a country's melodic literature are called "folklike" or "composed folk songs." Those by Stephen Foster can be cited as examples. Probably the best known of his compositions is "Old Folks at Home" (page 12), which is sung in many languages. This song can, in fact, be said to be universal in its appeal.

Art Songs

Songs thoughtfully composed by musicians and with accompaniments as a significant part of the composition are "art songs." They are sometimes "through composed;"[1] that is, the music follows the thought of the poem and changes from stanza to stanza in accordance with the meaning of the words. Folk songs, on the other hand, are strophical, with each stanza having the same melody. Composers of art songs also use the strophic form in some of their songs. See, for example, "The Little Sandman" (page 23) and "Lullaby" (page 14), both by Brahms, and "Wandering" (page 126), by Schubert.

Composers of the eighteenth and nineteenth centuries, notably Franz Schubert, brought the art song[2] to a state of perfection. As a songwriter, Robert Schumann probably ranks second only to Schubert. Johannes Brahms also was among those who composed exceptionally fine songs.

1. From the German *durchkomponiert.*
2. German art songs are called "lieder."

example of a strophic art song

THE SMITH

Ludwig Uhland

Johannes Brahms; Opus 19, No. 4

1. The black smith I hear, His hammer is bang - ing And clash - ing and clang - ing! A - far it re - sound - eth, Like
2. A strong man is he. His hammer is swing - ing, The an - vil is sing - ing, The bel - lows is spring - ing; The

church - bells   it   sound - eth,   so   loud_____
sparks   high   are   soar - ing   from   blows_____

_____ and   so   clear.
_____ firm   and   free.

f

149

THE TWO GRENADIERS

Friedrich Heine   Robert Schumann

To France were re - turn-ing two Gren - a-diers, Their Russ-ian cap-tiv-i-ty leav-ing; And when they came to the Ger-man fron-tiers, Their heads were bow'd down with

150

3. This dramatic art ballad tells of Napoleon's disastrous Russian campaign and of his defeat and captivity. Written by two Germans (Heine and Schumann), it nevertheless expresses the deep nationalistic feeling of the French. The music of the closing section is that of the French national anthem, "The Marseillaise."

griev - ing. 'Twas there that they both heard the sor - row - ful news; Dis -

as - ter their coun - try had shak - en. De - feat - ed and scat - ter'd that

val - i - ant host, And the Em - p'ror, the Em - p'ror was tak - en.

Then sor - row'd to - geth - er the gren - a - diers, Such dole - ful news to be

151

learn - ing; And then one spoke a - mid his tears, "Once more my old wounds are

burn - ing." The oth - er said, "The end has come; I would that I were dy - ing; But

I've a wife and child at home On me for bread re - ly - ing." "Who cares for

wife? Who cares for child? What mat - ter if they are for -

sak - en? Let them beg for bread if they hun - gry be; My

Em - p'ror, my Em - p'ror is tak - en! O grant me, broth - er, but one

pray'r: If I my hours must num - ber, Take

with thee my bod - y to France a - gain, And there let me calm - ly

Più mosso

slum - ber. My cross of hon - or with scar - let band

Leave o'er my bos - om ly - ing. My mus - ket place with - in my

hand, My sword a - round me ty - ing. So

thus will I lie with - in the tomb, A sen - try so still and un -

154

stir-ring, 'Till the roar of can-non re-sounds thro' the gloom And

tramp of the horse-men are spur-ring. Then ov-er my grave will my

Em-p'ror ride, with his sa-bre flash-ing in splen-dor, with sa-bre flash-ing in

splen-dor. Then armed for the fray will I rise from the grave, My

155

Em - p'ror, my Em - p'ror de - fend - ing."

Miscellaneous Classifications of Songs

In addition to folk and art songs, there are songs classified according to their words and uses, such as hymns, spirituals, carols, lullabies, love songs, patriotic songs, play or game songs, chanteys, work songs, ballads, and sacred, secular, popular, and classical songs.

Assignment

1. Review songs you have sung in this book and list two or three examples each of different types, such as folk, art, and ballad.

2. Sing the songs in this chapter, paying particular attention to the type of each.

3. Write brief musical discussions of "The Smith" by Brahms and "The Two Grenadiers" by Schumann (mode, mood, and so forth).

appendix

conducting A

Simply stated, the basic and traditional baton motions to show measure beats consist in freely moving the hand and arm down, up, left, and right as described on pages 20–21. The downbeat always shows the main accent or pulsation in a full measure of music. It is usually wise to learn these motions first without and then with a baton. A rhythm stick or pencil may serve as a substitute for the regular conducting baton. Use the hand and arm which are most natural to you. However, after a little practice you will be able to make the motions with either hand and with both hands simultaneously.

The concerns of a conductor are to show the beat, to start and stop the group together, and to indicate shadings in volume of tone and variations in tempo. As a rule, you give the basic beats with the right hand and the interpretative directions with your left. If you are left-handed, the movements are reversed. However, you need not always use the second hand for interpretative signs, for you can indicate them with the incisiveness of your beats.

Not all songs begin on the first beat of a measure; some have what is known as a "pickup" beat. It is important that you give the right movements for these. The song "America, the Beautiful," for example, begins on the last beat of a four-beat measure. Your motions, therefore, would be *up* for the beginning tone.

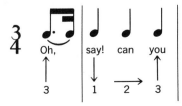

The song "The Star-Spangled Banner" begins on the third, or up, beat of a three-beat measure.

To ensure that a group makes the correct attack, with each singer beginning on the first word, you need to give a *preparatory* beat—a beat preliminary to the starting tone. Thus for "America," which begins on the first beat of a three-beat measure (the downbeat), the preparatory, or cue, beat is the last beat of an imaginary preceding measure, with the hand moving up.

In "The Star-Spangled Banner," the preparatory beat is the second beat, with the hand and arm moving toward the right (away from the body).

The preparatory beat should be distinct so that singers know exactly when to sing. You may at first find it difficult to give the cue beat, and you may have to resort to such devices as whispering or speaking the words "ready, sing." Or you may count the beats as "one, two, sing." The word *sing* should always be spoken on the cue, or preparatory, beat. However, you should discard these makeshifts as soon as possible.

the piano pedals B

The piano has either two or three pedals. The one on your right as you face the instrument is called the "damper" pedal. When it is lowered by a slight pressure of your right foot, it raises the damper of all the strings, leaving them free to vibrate. The resonance of tones is thereby increased. The pedal farthest to the left is called the "soft" pedal. When you press this down, it moves the hammers in such a way as to make the sound softer. In a grand piano, this pedal moves the entire action of the instrument (keys, dampers, etc.) sideways so that the hammers cannot make complete contact with the strings. In most upright or spinet pianos, the soft pedal moves the bank of hammers closer to the strings so that the keys have less force. When there are three pedals, the middle one is called the "sostenuto," or sustaining, pedal. When it is depressed, it keeps raised only those dampers associated with the keys which are being played.

When used properly, the damper pedal ensures smoothly connected tones of rich and resonant quality. But if it is not used correctly, the sounds become blurred and unpleasant. As a rule, this pedal should be pressed with lightning quickness after the notes are played. It should be released just as speedily with the change in harmony. Never make the mistake of using it as a footrest and keeping your foot on it throughout even a simple composition.

writing musical notation C

Casual observation of the musical score may be enough to enable some of you to write musical symbols, but others may need specific directions. In either case, you must take care to place the symbols accurately. In copying songs, you may write the words first under the staff and then divide the staff into measures before placing the notation. You may, however, prefer to write the music first and then place the words under the notes. Whichever method you select, be sure to leave plenty of space between syllables and words or notes so that your copy is exact.

G Clef

The G clef can be made in two strokes. First, draw a straight line from the space above the staff to the one below, finishing it with a slight upward turn to the left.

Second, make a small half circle from the top to the right of the straight line. Cross it at the fourth degree line and curve it to the left, bringing it to the first staff line. Now swing it around the second line (G).

F Clef

You start the F-clef sign with a good-sized dot on the fourth line of the staff. Carry it to the fifth line and then curve it to the second line. It somewhat resembles a C written backward. Place two dots on either side of the fourth line (F).

Notes

Notes consist of heads and stems and, in some cases, flags (sometimes called "hooks"). To write the heads of whole and half notes, make two small curved lines (⌢, ○). The heads of quarter notes and those of lesser value are made with a heavy stroke of the pen or with a swirling motion of the pencil (♩ ♩). When writing on the chalkboard, the solid, or filled, notes are made by moving the chalk diagonally (♩). The stems are turned up on the right side of notes when they are below the third line of the staff and are turned down on the left when they are above the third line.

The stem of a single note on the third line may be either up or down. The stem is usually down if that of the next note is down; it is up if the stem of the next note is up.

When a note on the third line is slurred to a preceding note, the stem takes the direction of that note.

Flags or hooks are on the right of notes regardless of whether the stems are up or down.

However, when an eighth note and those of lesser value are connected by a bar (beam), the flag is to the left if the eighth note comes first.

Bars (beams) connecting notes are at an angle when notes are on different degrees of the staff.

Rests

A whole rest is a short bar placed below the fourth line of the staff.

A half rest is a short bar placed above the third line of the staff.

The quarter rest is something like the letter Z reversed ( ). However, in printed music the symbol for the quarter rest is . An eighth rest resembles the number 7 ( ). To make rests of lesser value, add one or more flags to the eighth rest (sixteenth rest, ; thirty-second rest,).

The Dot

The dot is placed on a space after the note which it affects.

Sharps, Flats, and the Natural

To draw the sharp, make two vertical lines (‖) and then make two lines slanting upward from left to right (⚌♯). The double sharp looks like the letter X (✕).

To draw the flat, make a downstroke, retrace it approximately halfway, and make a curved line joining it to the bottom of the straight line (│♭). The double flat consists of two flats placed close together (♭♭).

The natural is made in two strokes: a line down and a short diagonal line up, a short diagonal line up and a straight line down (♮ ♮).

Key Signatures

Sharps and flats are placed in the order of keys and on the exact line or space to which they belong.

Meter Signatures

The meter signature is placed after the key signature. The upper number is above the third line, and the lower number is below it.

Segno

This symbol is like a capital S—sometimes with a line drawn through it (𝄋), sometimes with dots on either side (𝄋).

glossary of musical terms and symbols

Symbols

A double bar or a single heavy bar with either two or four dots indicates that a section of the music is to be repeated. If the repeat marks occur at only one point, the entire preceding part is to be repeated. If the marks occur twice, the section thus enclosed is to be repeated.

This indicates that a different ending is to be used for the repetition.

D.C.   (Da Capo) Means literally "from the head" and indicates that the repeat is to be from the beginning.

D.S.   (Dal Segno) Indicates a repetition from the sign 𝄋.

Fine   The end.

This is a fermata (hold). When placed over or under a note or rest, it means that these are to be prolonged beyond their usual time value. The exact length depends on the character of the music and the musical judgment of the performer or conductor.

A dot over or under a note is a "staccato" mark. It means that a note is to be sounded, then quickly released.

A tie is a curved line connecting two notes on the same degree of the staff. It means that only one tone is to be sounded but that this tone has a duration equal to the combined value of the notes.

A slur is a short curved line which shows that a syllable or a word is to be sung to two different pitches.

A curved line drawn over a group of notes means that these notes are to be sung smoothly (legato). It also indicates a phrase in music.

A brace connects the G and F staffs.

    sf   Means that the note is to be emphasized or stressed.

A bar or beam is a heavy line which connects the stems of eighth notes and those of lesser value.

Terms Relating to Vocal Music

A cappella   Choral music sung without instrumental accompaniment. The term literally means "in chapel style."

Aria   A solo found in operas and oratorios.

Art song   A song by a known composer in which the words, melody, and accompaniment reinforce each other, all being important.

Ballad   A song in which the words tell a story.

Canon   A contrapuntal or polyphonic (many voices) composition in which one part repeats what another part has sung. The imitation may be exact at the unison, or it may be at another interval, such as the fifth. A canon at the unison in which all singers enter at regular intervals and go from beginning to end as many times as desired is a "round."

Cantata   A composition with recitatives, arias, and choruses. The text may be either secular or religious.

Carol   A song of joy, praise, or devotion, usually sung in connection with Christmas, Easter, or other festive occasions.

Chantey   A song sung by sailors in rhythm with their work.

Chorale   A hymn tune of the German Protestant Church, dignified in character and sung at a slow tempo.

Descant or Discant   In present-day usage, a harmonizing melody added to a given melody and sung by a few soprano voices.

Folk song   A song of simple structure, the exact source of which is unknown. Sometimes a simple song by a known composer which has become a traditional part of a country's song literature is also classified as a folk song.

Madrigal   A contrapuntal part song popular in the sixteenth and seventeenth centuries.

Obbligato   An accompanying instrumental part (such as a violin obbligato).

Opera   A drama or play set to music. In grand opera, the plot is usually serious and with elaborate settings. Comic opera, with light and amusing libretto, often has speech mixed with song.

Operetta   A light, gay mixture of solos, choruses, and speaking parts.

Oratorio   A composition based on a religious text for soloists, chorus, and orchestra and performed without scenery or action.

Recitative   A vocal declamation found in operas and oratorios.

Round   See Canon.

Spiritual   A religious song of the American Negro, usually of deep pathos and beauty.

Terms to Indicate Tempo

Adagio   Slow

Andante   Moderately slow; literally, "going" or "walking"

Andantino   A little faster than andante

Allegretto   Moderately fast; a diminution of allegro

Allegro   Fast

Grave   Slowly and solemnly

Larghetto   Slightly faster than largo

Largo   Very slow

Lento   Slow

Moderato   Moderate

Prestissimo	Very fast
Presto	Fast
Vivace	Lively, quick

Terms to Indicate Change of Tempo

A tempo	Return to the original tempo
Accelerando	Accelerating, becoming faster
Allargando	Gradually growing slower and broadening the time
Meno mosso	Less motion, slower
Piu mosso	More motion, faster
Rallentando	Slowing down
Ritardando	Slow down, retard

Terms to Indicate Volume of Sound

Crescendo (*cresc.*, <)	Growing louder
Decrescendo (*decresc.* or *decr.*, >)	Growing softer
Diminuendo (*dim.*)	Diminishing in volume
Forte (f)	Loud
Fortissimo ($f\!f$)	Very loud
Mezzo forte (mf)	Medium loud
Mezzo piano (mp)	Medium soft
Pianissimo (pp)	Very soft
Piano (p)	Soft
Sforzando (sf)	A sudden increase of tone applied to single notes; with force or emphasis

Terms to Indicate Style

Agitato	Agitated
Animato	Animated
Brio	Brilliant, spirited
Dolce	Sweetly
Dolente	Grieving, sad
Energico	Energetically
Espressivo	Expressively
Forzo	Strong
Giocoso	Playfully, gaily
Grazioso	Gracefully
Legato	Smoothly, sustained
Leggiero	Lightly
Maestoso	Majestically
Marziale	Martially
Misterioso	Mysteriously
Pesante	Heavily
Portamento	Gliding from one tone to another
Risoluto	Resolutely
Scherzando	Playfully, jokingly
Sostenuto	Sustained
Staccato	Detached or separated—a style of performance in which the notes are more or less disconnected; the opposite of legato and sostenuto

$\frac{2}{2}$, $\frac{3}{4}$, $\frac{4}{4}$, and $\frac{6}{8}$ Measures

From *New Music Horizons*, Book Five. Copyright 1946, 1953, Silver Burdett Company, Morristown, N.J. Used by permission.

Elementary Song Series

American Singer, 2d ed., American Book Company, New York, 1959.
Birchard Music Series, Summy-Birchard Company, Evanston, Ill., 1962.
Discovering Music Together, Follett Publishing Company, Chicago, 1966.
Exploring Music, Holt, Rinehart and Winston, Inc., New York, 1966.
Growing with Music, Prentice-Hall, Inc., Englewood Cliffs, N.J., 1963.
The Magic of Music, Ginn and Company, Boston, 1964.
Making Music Your Own, Silver Burdett Company, Morristown, N.J., 1965.
Music for Living, Silver Burdett Company, Morristown, N.J., 1956.
Music for Young Americans, American Book Company, New York, 1959.
Our Singing World, enlarged ed., Ginn and Company, Boston, 1959.
This Is Music, Allyn and Bacon, Inc., Boston, 1962.
Together We Sing, rev. ed., Follett Publishing Company, Chicago, 1959.

Instruction Books for Classroom Instruments
wind instruments

Buchtel, Forest: *Melody Fun for Singing and Playing the Tonette,* Neil A. Kjos Company, Park Ridge, Ill., 1939.
Earle, Frederick: *Music Time for Flutophone and Other Pre-band Instruments,* Trophy Products Company, Cleveland, Ohio, 1961.
Enjoy Your Recorder, The Trapp Family Singers New Complete Method of Instruction for the Recorder, Magnamusic Distributors, Inc., Sharon, Conn., 1954.
Goodyear, Stephen: *The New Recorder Tutor Books,* Mills Music, Inc., New York, 1956.
Melody Method for Pre-instruments: Flutophone, Tonette, Song Flute, Recorder, Carl Fischer, Inc., New York, 1953.
Taylor, Maurice D., and Clement Wiedinmeyer: *Easy Steps for Melody Instruments,* Mills Music, Inc., New York, 1950.
Weber, Fred: *First Division Melody Instrument Method,* Belwin, Inc., New York, 1964.
White, Florence, and Anni Bergman: *Playing the Recorder,* Edward B. Marks Music Corporation, New York, 1965.

ukulele

Ball, Don: *You Can Play the Ukulele,* Associated Music Publishers, Inc., New York, 1950.
Bay, Mel: *Fun with the Ukulele,* Mel Bay Publications, Kirkwood, Mo., 1961.
Reser, Harry: *Let's Play the Uke,* Remick Music Corporation, New York, 1959.
Royal, Dan J.: *Instant Method for the Ukulele,* Ashley Publications, Inc., New York, 1965.
Sneck, Roy: *Simplified Ukulele Instruction,* David Gornston, New York, 1950.
Wolff's Ukulele Method, M. M. Cole Publishing Company, Chicago, 1955.

NOW THE DAY IS OVER

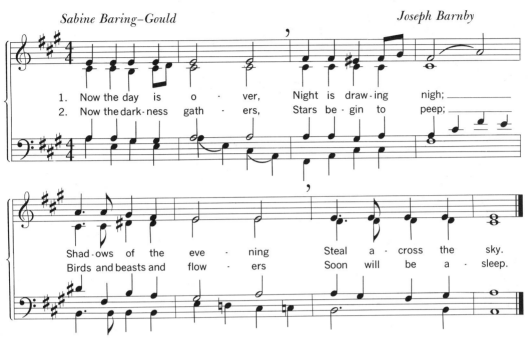

Sabine Baring-Gould   Joseph Barnby

1. Now the day is o - ver, Night is draw - ing nigh;
2. Now the dark - ness gath - ers, Stars be - gin to peep;

Shad - ows of the eve - ning Steal a - cross the sky.
Birds and beasts and flow - ers Soon will be a - sleep.

ALL THROUGH THE NIGHT

Welsh

Quietly

1. Sleep, my child and peace at - tend thee All through the night,
2. While the moon her watch is keep - ing All through the night,

Guard - ian an - gels God will send thee All through the night,
While the wea - ry world is sleep - ing All through the night,

169

Soft the drow-sy hours are creep-ing, Hill and vale in slum - ber steep-ing,
O'er thy spir - it gent - ly steal-ing, Vi - sions of de - light re - veal-ing,

I my lov - ing vig - il keep-ing All through the night.
Breathes a pure and ho - ly feel-ing All through the night.

JOY TO THE WORLD

Isaac Watts
Joyfully

George F. Handel
Arranged by Lowell Mosan

1. Joy to the world! The Lord is come; Let earth re - ceive her King; ___
2. Joy to the world! The Sav - iour reigns; Let men their songs em - ploy, ___

Let ev - 'ry ___ heart ___ pre - pare ___ Him ___ room ___
While fields and ___ floods, ___ rocks, hills, ___ and ___ plains ___

170

And heav'n and na - ture ___ sing, And ___ heav'n and na - ture ___
Re - peat the sound - ing ___ joy, Re - peat the sound - ing ___

sing, And ___ heav'n, and heav'n ___ and na - ture sing.
joy, Re ___ peat, re - peat ___ the sound - ing joy.

THE BLUE BELLS OF SCOTLAND

Annie McVicar   Old Scotch Air
Moderately

1. O where, and O where is your High-land lad - die gone? O where, and O
2. O where, and O where does your High-land lad - die dwell? O where, and O

where is your Highland lad - die gone? He's gone to fight the foe for King
where does your Highland lad - die dwell? He dwelt in mer - ry Scot-land, at the

cresc.

George up - on the throne; And it's oh! in my heart how I wish him safe at home!
sign of the Blue Bell; And it's oh! in my heart that I love my lad - die well.

171

VESPER HYMN

Thomas Moore

Attributed to D. Bortniansky

Hark, the ves - per hymn is steal - ing O'er the wa - ters soft and clear.
Near - er yet and near - er peal - ing, Soft it breaks up - on the ear.

Ju - bi - la - te! Ju - bi - la - te! Ju - bi - la - te! A----- men.

MAY DAY CAROL

English Folk Song from Essex County

Tenderly

1. The moon shines bright, The stars give light, A lit - tle be - fore it's day. Our
2. A - wake, a - wake, O pretty, pretty maid, Out of ___ your drow - sy dream, And

Heav - en - ly Fa - ther, He called to us And bid us to wake and pray.
step ___ in - to your ___ dair - y shed And fetch me a bowl of cream.

3. If not a bowl of your sweet cream,
   A cup to bring you cheer;
   For I don't know if we'll meet again,
   To be maying another year.

4. For I've been ramb'ling all this night
   And on into this day;
   And now, returning back again,
   I bring you a branch of May.

5. A branch of May I bring you here,
   As at your door I stand.
   'Tis but a sprout well budded out,
   The work of our dear Lord's hand.

6. My song is done, I must be gone.
   No longer can I stay.
   God bless you all, both great and small,
   And send you a joyful May.

172

From *Music Near and Far.* Copyright 1956, Silver Burdett Company, Morristown, N.J. Used by permission.

SLUMBER BOAT

Alice C. D. Riley

Music by Jessie L. Gaynor

Back a-gain to me.

DRINK TO ME ONLY WITH THINE EYES

Ben Jonson   *Old English Air*

1. Drink to me on - ly with thine eyes, And I will pledge with mine;
2. I sent thee late a ro - sy wreath, Not so much hon'ring thee

Or leave a kiss with - in the cup, And I'll not ask for wine; The
As giv - ing it a hope that there It could not wither'd be; But

thirst that from the soul doth rise, Doth ask a drink di - vine;
thou there - on didst on - ly breathe, And send'st it back to me,

But might I of Jove's nec - tar sip, I would not change for thine.
Since when it grows and smells, I swear, Not of it - self, but thee.

174

SWEET NIGHTINGALE

Old English Air

Allegro grazioso

1. Pret - ty maid, come a - long, Don't you hear the fond song, The sweet notes of the
2. Pret - ty Bet - ty, don't fail, For I'll car - ry your pail Safe ____ home to your
3. Pray, ____ let me a - lone, I have hands of my own; A ____ long with you,

night - in - gale flow? _____ Don't you hear the fond tale Of the sweet night - in -
cot as we go; _____ You shall hear the fond tale Of the sweet night - in -
Sir, I'll not go _____ To ____ hear the fond tale of the sweet night - in -

cresc.   *dim.*

gale As she sings in the val - ley be - low _____
gale As she sings in the val - ley be - low _____
gale As she sings in the val - ley be - low _____

mf

_____ As she sings in the val - ley be - low?
_____ As she sings in the val - ley be - low?
_____ As she sings in the val - ley be - low.

175

THE TREE IN THE WOOD[1]

English Folk Song

1. All in a wood there grew a tree, The fin-est tree you ev-er did see,
2. And on this tree there grew a limb, The fin-est limb you

And the green leaves grew a-round, a-round, a-round, And the green leaves grew a-round.

ev-er did see; The limb was on the tree, The tree was in the wood,

Refrain

And the green leaves grew a-round, a-round, a-round, And the green leaves grew a-round.

176

3. And on this limb there was a branch,
   The finest branch you ever did see,
   The branch was on the limb,
   The limb was on the tree,
   The tree was in the wood,
   And the green leaves grew all around, etc.

4. And on this branch there was a nest, etc.
5. And in this nest there was an egg, etc.
6. And in this egg there was a bird, etc.
7. And on this bird there was a wing, etc.
8. And on this wing there was a feather, etc.

1. As each object is named in each stanza, those named previously are repeated in reverse order until the song is completed.

O REST IN THE LORD
(*From the oratorio "Elijah"*)

Adapted from Psalm XXXVII   *Felix Mendelssohn*

O rest in the Lord, wait pa-tient-ly for Him, and He shall give thee thy heart's de - sires. O rest in the Lord, wait pa - tient-ly for Him, and He shall give thee thy heart's de - sires, and He shall give thee thy heart's de - sires. Com - mit thy way un - to Him, and trust in Him; com - mit thy way un -

177

to Him, and trust in Him, and fret not thy - self because of e - vil do - ers. O rest in the Lord, wait pa - tient - ly for Him, wait pa - tient - ly for Him; O rest in the Lord, wait pa - tient - ly for Him, and He shall give thee thy heart's de - sires, and He shall give thee thy heart's de - sires, and He shall

give thee thy heart's de-sires. O rest in the Lord, O rest in the

Lord, and wait, wait pa-tient-ly for Him.

OLD FOLKS AT HOME

Stephen C. Foster

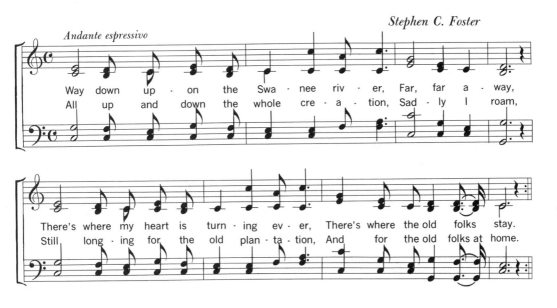

Way down up-on the Swa-nee riv-er, Far, far a-way,
All up and down the whole cre-a-tion, Sad-ly I roam,

There's where my heart is turn-ing ev-er, There's where the old folks stay.
Still long-ing for the old plan-ta-tion, And for the old folks at home.

179

All the world is sad and drear - y, Ev - 'ry - where I roam;

Oh, how my heart grows sad and wear - y, Far from the old folks at home.

AMERICA

Samuel Francis Smith

Henry Carey

1. My coun - try, 'tis of thee, Sweet land of lib - er - ty, Of thee I sing;
2. My na - tive coun - try, thee, Land of the no - ble free, Thy name I love;

Land where my fa - thers died, Land of the Pil - grims' pride,
I love thy rocks and rills, Thy woods and tem - pled hills;

From ev - 'ry ___ moun - tain - side, Let ___ free - dom ring.
My heart with ___ rap - ture thrills Like ___ that a - bove.

180

3. Let music swell the breeze,
And ring from all the trees
Sweet Freedom's song;
Let mortal tongues awake,
Let all that breathe partake,
Let rocks their silence break,
The sound prolong.

4. Our fathers' God, to Thee,
Author of liberty,
To Thee we sing;
Long may our land be bright
With Freedom's holy light;
Protect us by Thy might,
Great God, our King.

THE LITTLE SANDMAN

Johannes Brahms

1. The flow-ers all are sleep-ing be-neath the moon's bright ray; They nod their heads to-geth-er and dream _ the night _ a - way. The bud-ding trees wave to and fro and mur-mur soft and low.

2. Now, see, at ev-'ry win-dow the sand-man shows his head And looks for lit-tle chil-dren who ought _ to be _ in bed And, _ as each sleep-y one he spies, throws dust in-to his eyes.

Refrain

Sleep _ on, sleep _ on, _ sleep _

181

on, my lit - tle one.   one.

FLOW GENTLY, SWEET AFTON

Robert Burns   *James E. Spilman*

1. Flow gen - tly, sweet Af - ton, a - mang thy green braes; Flow gen - tly I'll sing thee a
2. How lof - ty, sweet Af - ton, thy neigh - bor - ing hills, Far mark'd with the cours - es of

182

song in thy praise; My Ma - ry's a - sleep by thy mur - mur - ing stream, Flow gen - tly, sweet
clear wind - ing rills! There dai - ly I wan - der, as morn ris - es high, My flocks and my

Af - ton, dis - turb not her dream. Thou stock - dove, whose ech - o re - sounds from the
Ma - ry's sweet cot in my eye. How pleas - ant thy banks and green val - leys be -

hill, Ye wild whist - ling black - birds in yon thor - ny dell, Thou green crest - ed
low, Where wild in the wood - lands the prim - ros - es blow, There oft, as mild

lap - wing, thy scream - ing for - bear; I charge you, dis - turb not my slum - ber - ing fair
eve - ning creeps o - ver the lea, The sweet scent - ed birk shades my Ma - ry and me.

GOD REST YOU MERRY, GENTLEMEN

Traditional

English Carol

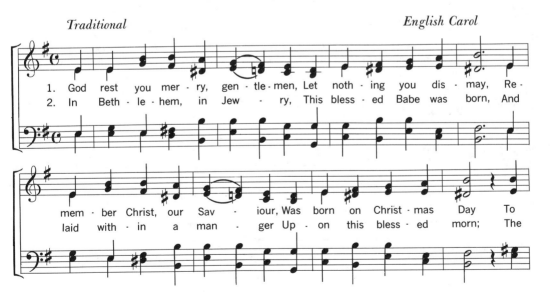

1. God rest you mer - ry, gen - tle - men, Let noth - ing you dis - may, Re -
2. In Beth - le - hem, in Jew - ry, This bless - ed Babe was born, And

mem - ber Christ, our Sav - iour, Was born on Christ - mas Day To
laid with - in a man - ger Up - on this bless - ed morn; The

183

save us all from Sa - tan's pow'r When we were gone a - stray.
which His moth - er Ma ry did noth - ing take in scorn. O _____

ti - dings of com - fort and joy, com - fort and

joy, O _____ ti - dings of com - fort and joy.

THE STAR-SPANGLED BANNER

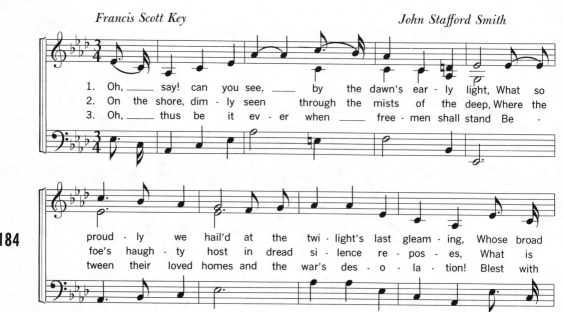

Francis Scott Key   *John Stafford Smith*

1. Oh, _____ say! can you see, _____ by the dawn's ear - ly light, What so
2. On the shore, dim - ly seen through the mists of the deep, Where the
3. Oh, _____ thus be it ev - er when _____ free - men shall stand Be -

184

proud - ly we hail'd at the twi - light's last gleam - ing, Whose broad
foe's haugh - ty host in dread si - lence re - pos - es, What is
tween their loved homes and the war's des - o - la - tion! Blest with

stripes and bright stars, through the per - il - ous fight, O'er the ram - parts we
that which the breeze, o'er the tow - er - ing steep As it fit - ful - ly
vic - t'ry and peace, may the heav'n - res - cued land Praise the Pow'r that hath

watch'd were so gal - lant - ly stream - ing? And the rock - ets' red glare, the bombs
blows, half con - ceals, half dis - clos - es? Now it catch - es the gleam of the
made and pre - served us a na - tion! Then ___ con - quer we must, for our

burst - ing in air, Gave ___ proof through the night that our
morn - ing's first beam, In full glo - ry re - flect - ed now ___
cause it is just, And ___ this be our mot - to: "In ___

Chorus

flag was still there. Oh, ___ say, does that ___ Star - span - gled Ban - ner ___ yet ___
shines on the stream. 'Tis the Star - span - gled ___ Ban - ner! Oh, long may ___ it ___
God is our trust." And the Star - span - gled ___ Ban - ner in tri - umph shall ___

wave ___ O'er the land ___ of the free and the home of the brave?
wave ___ O'er the land ___ of the free and the home of the brave!
wave ___ O'er the land ___ of the free and the home of the brave!

185

LULLABY

Johannes Brahms

1. Lul-la-by and good night! With ro-ses be-dight; Creep in-to thy bed, There pil-low thy head. If God will, thou shalt wake When the morn-ing doth break, If God will, thou shalt wake When the morn-ing doth break.

2. Lul-la-by and good night! Thy blue eyes close tight; Bright an-gels are near, So sleep with-out fear. They will guard thee from harm, With fair dream-land's sweet charm, They will guard thee from harm, With fair dream-land's sweet charm.

186

DIXIE

Daniel D. Emmett

1. I wish I was in the land of cot - ton, Old times there are not for - got - ten, Look a - way! Look a - way! Look a - way! Dix - ie Land. In Dix - ie Land where I was born in, Ear - ly on one fros - ty morn - ing, Look a - way! Look a - way! Look a - way! Dix - ie Land.

2. There's buck - wheat cakes and In - dian bat - ter Makes you fat or a lit - tle fat - ter, Look a - way! Look a - way! Look a - way! Dix - ie Land. Then hoe it down and scratch your grav - el, To Dix - ie Land I'm bound to trav - el, Look a - way! Look a - way! Look a - way! Dix - ie Land.

187

Refrain

Then I wish I was in Dix - ie, Hoo - ray! Hoo - ray! In Dix - ie Land I'll take my stand, To live and die in Dix - ie, A - way, A - way, A - way down south in Dix - ie, A - way, A - way, A - way down south in Dix - ie.

EVENING SONG

Carl Maria von Weber

Soft - ly sighs the breath of eve - ning,

Steal - ing through the shadow - y grove,

While the stars in hea - ven shin - ing

188

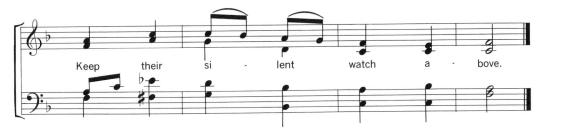

Keep their si - lent watch a - bove.

COCKLES AND MUSSELS

Old Irish Song

In Dub-lin's fair cit-y, where girls are so pret-ty, 'Twas there I first

met with sweet Mol-ly Ma-lone; She drove a wheel-bar-row through

streets broad and nar-row, Sing-ing "Cock-les and mus-sels, a-live, all a-live!"

189

A - live, a - live oh! ___ a - live, a - live oh! ___ Sing - ing "Cock - les and

mus - sels a - live, all a - live!" She died of the "fa - ver," and noth - ing could

save her, And that was the end of sweet Mol - ly Ma - lone; But her

ghost drives a bar - row through streets broad and nar - row, Sing - ing "Cock - les and

muslims a‑live, all a‑live!" A‑live, a‑live oh!___ a‑live, a‑live oh!___ Sing‑ing "Cock‑les and mus‑sels, a‑live, all a‑live!"

WE GATHER TOGETHER

Traditional Dutch Tune

Moderately

1. We gath‑er to‑geth‑er to ask the Lord's bless‑ing; He
2. Be‑side us to guide us, our God with us join‑ing, Or‑

chas‑tens and has‑tens His will to make known. The
dain‑ing, main‑tain‑ing His king‑dom di‑vine. So

wick‑ed op‑press‑ing, now cease___ from dis‑tress‑ing. Sing
from the be‑gin‑ning, the fight___ we were win‑ning, Thou,

191

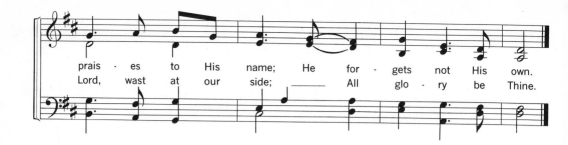

praises to His name; He forgets not His own.
Lord, wast at our side; ___ All glory be Thine.

BATTLE HYMN OF THE REPUBLIC

Julia Ward Howe   *William Steffe*

1. Mine eyes have seen the glory of the coming of the Lord; He is
2. I have seen Him in the watch-fires of a hundred circling camps; They have

trampling out the vintage where the grapes of wrath are stor'd; He hath loos'd the fateful
builded Him an altar in the evening dews and damps; I can read His righteous

lightning of His terrible swift sword; His truth is marching on.
sentence by the dim and flaring lamps; His day is marching on.

192

Chorus

Glory, glory, Hallelujah! Glory, glory, Hallelujah!

Glo - ry, glo - ry, Hal - le - lu - jah! His truth is march - ing on.

WHEN JOHNNY COMES MARCHING HOME

Louis Lambert

With Spirit

1. When John-ny comes march-ing home a-gain, Hur-rah, hur-rah! We'll give him a heart-y
2. Get rea-dy for the Ju-bi-lee, Hur-rah, hur-rah! We'll give the he-ro

wel-come then, Hur - rah, hur - rah! The men will cheer, the boys will shout, The
three times three, Hur - rah, hur - rah! The lau-rel wreath is rea-dy now To

Chorus

la - dies, they will all turn out, And we'll all feel gay, When John-ny comes march-ing home.
place up - on his loy - al brow,

193

SWEET AND LOW

Alfred, Lord Tennyson

Joseph Barnby

1. Sweet and low, sweet and low, Wind of the west-ern
2. Sleep and rest, sleep and rest, Fa-ther will come to thee

sea, _____ Low, low, breathe and blow,
soon, _____ Rest, rest on moth-er's breast,

Wind of the west-ern sea, _____ O-ver the roll-ing
Fa-ther will come to thee soon. _____ Fa-ther will come to his

wa - ters go, Come from the dy - ing moon and blow;
babe in the nest, Sil - ver sails all out of the west;

Blow him a - gain to me, _____ While my lit - tle one,
Un - der the sil - ver moon, _____ Sleep, my lit - tle one,

While my pret - ty one sleeps. _____
Sleep, my pret - ty one, sleep. _____

195

SANTA LUCIA

Neapolitan Folk Song

Moderately

1. Now 'neath the sil - ver moon, o - cean is glow - ing, O'er the calm bil - low
   Here balm - y breez - es blow, pure joys in - vite us, And as we gent - ly row,

2. When o'er thy wa - ters light winds are play - ing, Thy spell can soothe us,
   To thee, sweet Na - po - li, what charms are giv - en, Where smiles cre - a - tion,

soft winds are blow - ing;
all things de - light us.
all care al - lay - ing;
Home of fair Po - e - sy, Realm of pure
toil blest by heav - en.

Refrain

Hark, how the sail - or's cry Joy - ous - ly
Home of fair Po - e - sy, Realm of pure

ech - oes nigh: San - ta Lu - ci - a! San - ta Lu - ci - a!
Har - mo - ny, San - ta Lu - ci - a! San - ta Lu - ci - a!

HERE WE COME A-WASSAILING

Traditional

Brightly

1. Here we come a - was - sail - ing a - mong the leaves so green; ___
2. We are not dai - ly beg - gars that beg from door to door, ___ But
3. God bless the mas - ter of this house like - wise the mis - tress, too; ___ And

Here we come a-wan-d'ring, so fair_____ to be seen.
we are neigh-bors' chil-dren whom you have seen be-fore.
all the lit-tle chil-dren that round the ta-ble go.

f Refrain

Love and joy come to you, and to you your was-sail, too; And God bless you and

send you a hap-py New Year, And God send you a hap-py New Year!

TWELVE DAYS OF CHRISTMAS

Old English Folk Song

On the first day of Christ-mas, my true love sent to me A

par - tridge in a pear tree. 2. On the sec - ond day of Christ - mas, my
3. On the third day of Christ - mas, my
4. On the fourth day of Christ - mas, my

true love sent to me Two tur - tle doves And a par - tridge in a pear
true love sent to me Three French hens
true love sent to me Four col - ly birds

tree. 5. On the fifth day of Christ - mas, my true love sent to me

Five gol - den rings, Four col - ly birds, Three French hens,

Two tur-tle doves, and a par-tridge in a pear tree.

6. On the sixth day of Christ-mas, my true love sent to me
7. On the seventh day of Christ-mas, my true love sent to me
8-12.

Six geese a-lay-ing, Five gol-den rings, Four col-ly birds,
Seven swans a-swim-ming,

Three French hens, Two tur-tle doves, and a par-tridge in a pear tree.

199

8. On the eighth day . . .
    Eight maids a-milking; . . .

9. On the ninth day . . .
    Nine ladies dancing; . . .

10. On the tenth day . . .
    Ten lords a-leaping; . . .

11. On the eleventh day . . .
    Eleven pipers piping; . . .

12. On the twelfth day of Christmas,
    My true love sent to me
    Twelve drummers drumming, Eleven pipers piping,
    Ten lords a-leaping, Nine ladies dancing,
    Eight maids a-milking, Seven swans a-swimming,
    Six geese a-laying, Five golden rings,
    Four colly birds, Three French hens,
    Two turtle doves, and a partridge in a pear tree.

THE ORGAN-GRINDER[2]

Wilhelm Müller

Franz Schubert

Up be-hind the vil-lage stands an or-gan man, And with stiff-en'd fin-gers turns as best he can;

2. With "The Organ-grinder," Schubert ends his cycle "The Winter Journey." A song cycle is a group of songs related in mood or with a continuous story. The song pictures the bleakness of winter and the poor old organ-grinder with stiffened fingers playing his melancholy tune. Notice the drone bass A, with its fifth tone above throughout the accompaniment. The organ-grinder's two-bar tune enters intermittently.

This cycle tells of a wandering, lonely man seeking solace in nature. He finally meets and links his fate with the organ-grinder. The two disappear into the snowy landscape. It is said that this final song of the cycle presages the coming of Schubert's death and that in it he voiced the thought that only after he was gone would his music be heard.

On the cold ground, bare-foot, si-dles here and there,

And his emp-ty sau-cer shows the gifts are rare,

And his emp-ty sau-cer shows the gifts are rare.

No one lis-tens to him, no one looks or cares,

Snarl - ing dogs pur - sue him, still a smile he wears;

And no dis - ap - point-ment does he once be - tray,

But up - on the or - gan turns and turns a - way,

But up - on the or - gan turns and turns a - way.

Won·der·ful old min·strel,
shall I go with you?
Will you to my dit·ties
play the mu·sic, too? _____

* These notes may be sung an octave lower.

BESIDE THY CRADLE HERE I STAND

From Christmas Oratorio, by
Johann Sebastian Bach

Be - side Thy cra - dle here I stand, O Thou that ev - er liv - est, And bring Thee with a will - ing hand The ver - y gifts Thou giv - est. Ac - cept me; 'tis my mind and heart, My soul, my strength, my ev - 'ry part, That Thou from me re - quir - est.

GUARDIAN ANGELS

Robert Schumann; Opus 79, No. 21

1. When chil-dren lay them down to sleep, Two
2. But when they wake at dawn of day, The

an - gels come their watch to keep, Cov-'ring them up safe - ly and warm,
two bright an - gels go a - way, Rest - ing them from their work of love,

Ten-der-ly shield-ing them from harm.
For God Him-self keeps watch a - bove.

205

WANDERING[3]

Wilhelm Müller

Franz Schubert

Allegretto

mf

Fine

p

p

1. To wan - der is the mil - ler's ___ joy, To
2. The wa - ter long has taught us ___ this, The
3. We see it in the mill ___ wheels, too, The

mf 1.   2. *p*

wan - der,   To   He ___
wa - ter,   The   It ___
mill ___ wheels, We   They

mf

206

3.   This song, from the cycle "The Maid of the Mill," describes the young miller's delight in travel. The broken chords in the right hand and the repeated octaves in the left of the accompaniment depict the sprightly movement of the brook as it turns the mill wheel.

For greater ease in playing, the accompaniment has been transposed one octave above the original.

must a wretch - ed mil - ler _____ be Who _____
knows no rest by day - or _____ night, In _____
like not to be stand - ing _____ still, But _____

mf

nev - er cares the world _ to see, To wan - der, to _____
wan - d'ring al - ways takes _ de - light, The wa - ter, the _____
turn all day with right _ good will, The mill wheels, the _____

pp

D.C. al Fine

wan - der, to wan - der, to _____ wan - der.
wa - ter, the wa - ter, the _____ wa - ter.
mill wheels, the mill wheels, the _____ mill wheels.

pp

D.C. al Fine

207

AMERICA, THE BEAUTIFUL

Katharine Lee Bates   *Samuel A. Ward*

1. O beau-ti-ful for spa-cious skies, For am-ber waves of grain, For pur-ple moun-tain maj-es-ties A-bove the fruit-ed plain! A-mer-i-ca! A-mer-i-ca! God shed His grace on thee And crown thy good with broth-er-hood, From sea to shin-ing sea!

2. O beau-ti-ful for pil-grim feet, Whose stern im-pass-ion'd stress A thor-ough-fare for free-dom beat A-cross, the wil-der-ness! A-mer-i-ca! A-mer-i-ca! God mend thine ev-'ry flaw, Con-firm thy soul in self-con-trol, Thy lib-er-ty in law!

3. O beau-ti-ful for pa-triot dream,That sees be-yond the years, Thine al-a-bas-ter ci-ties gleam Un-dimm'd by hu-man tears! A-mer-i-ca! A-mer-i-ca! God shed His grace on thee And crown thy good with broth-er-hood, From sea to shin-ing sea!

DECK THE HALL

Welsh Carol

1. Deck the hall with boughs of hol-ly,
'Tis the sea-son to be jol-ly,
Fa la la la la la la la la.

2. See the blaz-ing Yule be-fore us,
Strike the harp and join the cho-rus,
Fa la la la la la la la la.

Don we now our gay ap-par-el, Fa la la la la la la la la.
Fol-low me in mer-ry meas-ure, Fa la la la la la la la la.

Troll the an-cient Yule-tide car-ol, Fa la la la la la la la la.
While I tell of Yule-tide treas-ure, Fa la la la la la la la la.

LONGING FOR SPRING

Wolfgang Amadeus Mozart

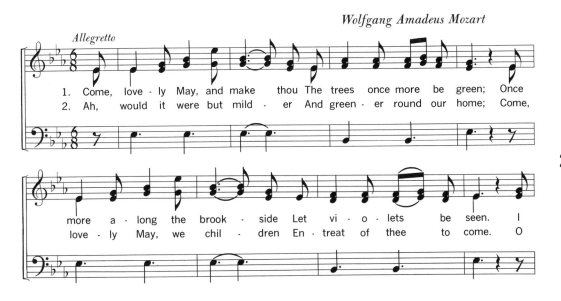

1. Come, love-ly May, and make thou The trees once more be green; Once
2. Ah, would it were but mild-er And green-er round our home; Come,

more a-long the brook-side Let vi-o-lets be seen. I
love-ly May, we chil-dren En-treat of thee to come. O

long with ea - ger long - ing for vi - o - lets to grow; Ah,
come, all wood and mea - dow, with vi - o - lets' per - fume; Bid

love - ly May, how glad - ly A - walk - ing I would go.
night - in - gale and cuck - oo Their wel - come notes re - sume.

TIT WILLOW

W. S. Gilbert

Sir Arthur Sullivan
From "The Mikado"

1. On a tree by a riv - er a lit - tle tom - tit Sang
2. He slapp'd at his chest as he sat on the bough, Sing - ing
3. Now I feel just as sure as I'm sure that my name Is - n't

"Wil - low, tit - wil - low, tit - wil - low." And I
"Wil - low, tit - wil - low, tit - wil - low." And a
wil - low, tit - wil - low, tit - wil - low, That 'twas

said to him, "Dick - y - bird, why do you sit, Sing - ing
cold per - spi - ra - tion be - span - gled his brow, "Oh,
blight - ed af - fec - tion that made him ex - claim, "Oh,

210

wil - low, tit - wil - low, tit - wil - low? Is it
wil - low, tit - wil - low, tit - wil - low." He
wil - low, tit - wil - low, tit - wil - low." And if

weak - ness of in - tel - lect, bird - ie" I cried, "Or a
sobb'd, and he sigh'd And a gur - gle he gave; Then he
you re - main cal - lous and ob - du - rate, I shall

rath - er tough worm in your lit - tle in - side?" With a
plung'd him - self in - to the bil - low - y wave, And an
per - ish as he did, and you will know why; Though I

shake of his poor lit - tle head, he re - plied, "Oh,
ech - o a - rose from the su - i - cide's grave, "Oh,
prob - a - bly shall not ex - claim as I die, "Oh,

wil - low, tit - wil - low, tit - wil - low."
wil - low, tit - wil - low, tit - wil - low."
wil - low, tit - wil - low, tit - wil - low."

211

THE FIRST PRIMROSE[4]

J. Paulsen   *Edvard Hagerup Grieg*

4.   This delicate, graceful song by Norway's most characteristic composer tells about the delight which the primrose brings as the first token of spring after the long, dreary Scandinavian winter. It should be sung with flowing, flexible rhythm and cheerful tone.

Spring is love-li-er than all, The time___ of love___ and play.___ For thee and me, O dear-est maid, The light of Spring is glow-ing; Then take___ the flow'r and rap-ture yield; Thy heart on me___ be-stow - ing.

213

indexes

song index

subject index